WITH LYRE, HARP AND A FLATPICK:

The Folk Musician at Worship

With Lyre, Harp...
and a Flatpick

The Folk Musician at Worship

Ed Gutfreund

NORTH AMERICAN LITURGY RESOURCES • CINCINNATI

First Printing: December 1973

Printed in the United States of America

TO MY FAMILY

Give thanks to the Lord on the harp;
With ten string lyre chant his praises.
Sing to him a new song;
    Pluck the strings skillfully,
    with shouts of gladness.

Author's Acknowledgements

If there is one thing I know, it is that this work would never have come about without many people's help. A few of them deserve recognition in print.

My parents, brothers and sisters, have made me aware of music and an ongoing harmony we experience together. They help me know freedom and direction and what it is like to be part of an outstanding family — I guess they are why I believe we can become a community of men.

Giles Pater and Jack Dreese — priests and teachers par excellence — without their patience and support my life experiences would have been very limited.

George Gates is my friend. Working with him gives me a chance to know language, to know idealism, and to know honesty.

Tom DiFolco, Zeke and Ginny Zimmerman, and Jim and Mary Brown are friends with whom I live. This household (which we somewhat presumptiously call the Eschatological Community) has been a welcome and needed base. We have rebuilt a house and now have a home to live in and invite friends to — and we celebrate every available occasion together. Their friendships are remarkable; I'm lucky to know them.

Phil Obermiller, Chris Hall and Eileen Frechette helped me believe I should keep writing, when I often felt like quitting.

Jack Berkemeyer, Skip Carsten, and Terry Place have been encouragements since my earliest musical-liturgical experiences. Their invitations to work, play, or sing have been invaluable, as well as their examples of priesthood.

Mike Zwertschek has been a long standing help with artistic ideas and offered early appreciation of the value of criticism.

Carol Young performed a miracle — she enabled me to get most of these thoughts on paper by her patient taking of dictation and her wizardry at the typewriter. I would never have finished without her help.

Erich Sylvester encouraged me to visit NALR — Ray Bruno and Dan Onley accepted and encouraged an initially vague idea. I appreciate their willingness to bear with uncertainty.

Finally, some friends who have helped me learn important aspects of music and life and have directly or indirectly influenced these pages — Bill Acosta, Louise Anderson, Valerie Blackmon, Sue Cassidy, Hersch and Joanie Conner, Bill Coulson, Pat Gates, Marcia Jaffe, John Marlowe, Mike Parmantie and Joe Wise . . . and many others who though not named are not forgotten.

Thank you all!

Ed Gutfreund

Table of Contents

The Author . . .

When North American Liturgy Resources was in its utter infancy several years ago, various people around Cincinnati repeatedly advised us to "get in touch with Ed Gutfreund." We needed all the good friends we could get, to be sure, but we never actually met the man for another two years. Yet we seemed to hear his name over and over again whenever the subjects of liturgical music, folksongs, workshops or the need for good new music came up.

Ed G. and NALR finally got acquainted in January of 1973. We were interested in his special knack for the "workshop" service for which we are so often asked — and we had gotten wind from Erich Sylvester that Ed's friends had finally succeeded in pressuring him to do the book they all knew he had in him.

Ed worked on the book through a good portion of 1973, frequently conducting or participating in workshops, large and small, sponsored by NALR. The rapport he develops so easily with any size group further convinced us that we had the right man working on a much-needed book.

After some years of conducting retreats, teacher-training sessions, liturgy and religious education work, and numerous other experiences which include serving on the staff of the annual LaJolla Institute, this widely-traveled folksinger/author/composer is back at the books preparing for ordained ministry in the Cincinnati Archdiocese. His love for and ability with folk music, from its early roots to its modern variations, is certain to enhance and strengthen his efforts to minister to the People, the folk, of God.

Introduction

by DAN F. ONLEY

Happily, there's a lot more to "Folk Music" for worship than the decade-old sound of a youthful group rendering a rigid 4/4 strum for a freedom song or an early composition by Ray Repp. In fact, there's been so much development and expansion of repertoire that a *description* of liturgical folk music, if not a *definition*, is becoming possible.

The thickest of hymnals could not contain even a tenth of the folk music being sung by Americans in their communal worship. This is because we are discovering, slowly and awkwardly, that we are, like the rest of the world, a musical people. Most of us appreciate and treasure the formal music of accomplished composers, but we are finding out, in spite of ourselves, that we can sing, that many of us can learn a familiar instrument, and that we can express both our hopes and our faith by writing or adapting songs.

And so we're writing original songs, setting Scripture passages to simple melodies, singing or borrowing from the ageless and

1

boundless wealth of American folk ballads, spirituals and hymns. We are rediscovering the songs of the Shakers, the native American, and the folk culture of our European and African forefathers. We bring to our celebrations those "popular" modern songs which mirror our religious concerns and hopes. Our usual instrumental accompaniment, though not exclusively so, is provided by the fundamental American instrument, the guitar.

Our songs are created or adapted for specific communities, often for certain and temporary occasions or themes. The songs come and go, change and develop; they number in the thousands. Certain songs have become known across the land by going through the publishing and recording process.

The formal publishing of folk-style music intended for our liturgical worship has been both a blessing and a curse on the American Church's strides over a decade to sing to God a new Canticle. We've been blessed with an availability of good prayerful music to all congregations. Composers with special talent have had the means to share the fruits of their work with the Church at large. These benefits must go hand in hand with the occasional publication of poor or artificial music and with the still-prevalent tendencies of music groups or congregations to seize upon a fixed collection of four or six songs, good or bad, and wear them out.

Acceptance by a publisher or pursuit of publication by a composer is not, or should not be, the ultimate destiny of a true folk song. Actual publication of a good song is, to be sure, an exciting event for both composer and those who thereby can become familiar with the song. The simple fact of publication, however, should never be taken to mean that a "published" song is necessarily better than an "unpublished" song. The important thing is that people at worship be enabled to sing prayerfully, regardless of where the songs for that particular congregation come from.

Time has passed. A lot of us hate to admit just how many years have gone by since we first experienced the Eucharistic celebration in English, or since we first sang the *Holy, Holy* or a song during Communion with guitar accompaniment. The TV networks shocked us this Fall with the reminder that ten years have passed since the murder of John F. Kennedy. As we begin to confront, with grimness, an era of restructuring lifestyles in the face of dwindling material resources we took for granted only a year ago, we recall that already five years have passed since that highly-charged era which also saw folk music for liturgy at an emotional peak of sorts. Martin Luther King . . . Robert Kennedy . . . Kent State . . . the burning of our cities . . . Resurrection City . . . in our pain and tension we could still somehow feel the Spirit movin' all over this land — and, Lord, how we could sing!

> *Mine eyes hath seen the glory of the*
> *coming of the Lord . . .*
> *Glory, glory halleluiah!!!*

Yes, how we could sing. We prayed in song for an end to the killing and fighting. Year after year we prayed and we sang. Today the popular or folk style of song in worship is no longer a novelty. We have new concerns about integrity in government and other broad social questions — and we have an ongoing and maturing concern over the depth and quality of our public worship, now that the new forms are comfortably familiar.

We are in a new phase or era for folk music in liturgy. Both composers and individual musicians are striving to serve the Church in ever better ways; old songs give way to newer ones which more perceptively speak out our hopes and our faith; the simple folk guitarist works hard to refine and expand the ability and talent he or she offers as gift to the Christian community.

For a variety of reasons, the guitar and folk/popular styles of singing are still despised by some. Other critics, attempting a benign tolerance, have seen it as a fad which would quietly fade away without so much as a last arpeggio.

We've got good news for the critics who have expected folk music to quietly go away. The *songs of the people* are stronger, more alive and beautiful than ever! A whole new tradition of truly singable songs and acclamations, faithful to the spirit of the Psalmist, Pope St. Gregory, and the monks of Solesmes is touching the faith-life of the people of, by, and for whom it has happened. Folk music, in its unique changeable, discardable and renewable manner, is here to stay, because the People are here to stay.

In this era of transition (which we hope will never end) there is much discontent with the state of church music. This kind of discontent is a sign of health and future possibility. One thing that must stop however, is the growing tendency of columnists to make folk music the total scapegoat for their frustration over the happy fact that the "new" liturgical music still has a lot of growing to do. Folk music and folk musicians are shrugged off, insulted, and blamed for all that is not satisfactory in liturgy today — by writers whose use of ten-dollar words should suggest a better total perspective on their part.

Like *any* kind of singing or music, folksong can indeed be done in a banal, trite and artless way. In addition to the rich new repertoire of worthwhile music which does exist, there is a corresponding wasteland of hackwritten stuff with guitar chords dubbed in, which not only is empty liturgically and musically, but which is not even truly "folk."

Badly-done music which involves guitars or a new style seems to turn people off more violently than do equally-poor music experiences in another style. Criticism, however, will always be the lot of something which is fresh or new. Women struggling for fair treatment in established professions voice the complaint that much more is demanded of them than of men in similar positions. The same is true for liturgical folk music — this is the pain and the price of change and growth. Folk music has to be done especially well, or it will have to face complaints and censures which even the most mediocre organist would never have to endure.

But why shouldn't all liturgical music — folk music included — be done as well and as beautifully and prayerfully as possible, all the time, and for all time? Today's folk musicians who serve the Church in worship deserve every bit as much respect and support as anybody else in the ministry of music — but I pray that none of them will ever be in a situation where poverty of content and effort is apathetically accepted.

Present-day folk musicians working with liturgy have a special new vantage point from which to take a good look at themselves. There is now a past as well as a present and the future. The time is ripe for a critical analysis of the use of folk music in the liturgical worship of the Church.

Such self-examination followed by learning and growth has already been happening by means of workshops and institutes. *WITH LYRE, HARP AND A FLATPICK* is the first book-length presentation of educational and critical help for the folk musician at worship. Ed Gutfreund has been part of the "movement" since its very beginning. The authenticity of both his musicianship and his pastoral perspectives, coupled with his book's timeliness, promise to make the following pages very helpful to any person seriously concerned about the musical, liturgical and pastoral worth of the songs we sing to the Lord in the years ahead.

The folk tradition in liturgical worship is growing out of its several early ills. Good taste and liturgical sensitivity suffered through a period which offered enough of the new-found "freedom" to play *anything* for worship . . . because it was different, neat, "relevant," or cool. Parishes are discovering that good music programs, while not financially burdensome, are definitely not free. As liturgy itself begins to receive budget consideration, so do the needs and efforts of the folk musicians who serve the parish. Parish liturgists are realizing that their problems with folk songs lay not with the songs themselves, but rather with what has been *done* to them. Familiar songs whose themes plugged into the "principal parts" of the Mass were horrendously overworked. Songs intended by their composers

5

for children were repeatedly foisted upon adults. The total burden of supplying both an instrument and also the music from which to play (or for the congregation to sing) has too often been left for the individual guitarist.

Parishes are learning to give their musicians the many kinds of help and support which they need to do their task as well as possible. Salaries, or at least stipends, are becoming more common, as are budgets for maintaining a parish music library, securing and paying for permissions to reprint music for the congregation, providing liturgical education, workshop attendance opportunities, music lessons and, yes, instruments for willing and faithful volunteers.

It's all happening at an opportune time, since the songs themselves have developed significantly in both quality and quantity. The way has been led, it seems, by two groups of people. 1) Many individual church musicians have composed new music for their own congregations who had outgrown the first crop of published liturgical songs. They have sought richer expressions of faith, more interesting musical style and have worked out successful integrations of folk-style music with other forms. 2) Recently-published collections of new composers (Sr. Suzanne Toolan, Joe Zsigray, Erich Sylvester, the monks of Weston Priory, John Foley and the other Jesuits at St. Louis, and others) have deeply enriched the repertoire. Two composers whose efforts and prominence date back to "the beginning" have made distinct individual contributions to the development of the songs themselves. The steady and measured output of new songs by Joe Wise paints a chronological picture of the direction being taken by new folk music. His five liturgical recordings, spanning 1966 to the present (1973) show a consistency in singability and content — but with a progressive refinement of musical and poetic expression and technique. Many would agree that his song *Lord, Teach Us to Pray* marked a turning-point in the history of folksong for prayer and worship by giving us all a concrete glimpse at the power, majesty, depth and potential of the medium. On the other hand, Fr. Carey Landry, whose *The Spirit is A-Movin'* belies the contention that folk music cannot have the durability of a classic, has assisted numerous groups in discovering the powerful beauty of singing itself, both through his own vast collection of music and his liberal use of many other songs. His approach in both composition and public presentation is doing much to dissolve the barriers erected between "folk" and "traditional" styles of church music.

All in all, the serious composing going on within the folk music field is proving to be very responsive to the liturgical needs of today. "Sub-styles" are emerging within the general genre of church-music-for-guitar.

The vocation or avocation of serving the Church's musical needs is being recognized as a ministry. Those who are able to offer the folk style of liturgical song to a congregation are faced today with new challenge and opportunity. Despite the critics, there is general acceptance of folk music in worship. We have a rich and broad repertoire of songs and settings from which to choose. We have a past from whose mistakes we certainly can learn. We are doing our work in an era which finds the Church actively appreciative of the role of music in its worship. We are in a position to be leaders, healers and reconcilers as well as musicians. We are in a terribly responsible position — the way we play and sing, what we sing, our attitude and our example all can affect the faith life of members of our congregations.

We're all fortunate, I believe, that this new book emerges at this particular time and that its author is Ed Gutfreund. Such a book three or five years ago would have been, however helpful, still premature. To wait much longer would be to deprive us all of some needed guidance and fresh perspective. Ed draws into his perspective not only his own extensive experience but also his many associations with others who have been active in the music and liturgical fields. We consider the book to be a major contribution to the ongoing efforts of North American Liturgy Resources to serve as the most productive and dependable influence for growth and fresh life in folk music for liturgy on this continent.

Author's Preface

About seven years ago, I invested what little money I could scrape together in a guitar. Many of my friends had been playing for some years and it looked like I might also learn to strum a few chords (although the possibility of simultaneously singing and playing seemed at that point an accomplishment of coordination beyond my wildest dreams). When I finally got the guitar and a copy of some "Eighty-three Thousand Easy Chords for All the Concertos of the World and Some of the Folk Tunes" book, I began to wonder what I had really done with that thirty-five dollars I spent. Having grown up with a basic attitude of "I spent it, so I might as well get something out of it," I practiced, and was amazed that even though I had not learned all eighty-three thousand of those easy chords, playing music was beginning to come more easily.

Eight guitars later I feel the same way about writing as I did initially about playing the guitar. Who ever thought about writing about musical experiences, especially those often connected with liturgical guitar picking? My purpose here is to bring together all the different questions, techniques, and suggestions which have given me the chance to pick a little better, or to help someone else pick a little better. Most of all I want to bring together those things we are all looking for to make us better able to lead our brothers and sisters in good music — music that will contribute to our ability to worship and express our faith more clearly.

With Lyre, Harp
and a Flatpick:
The
Folk
Musician
at
Worship

As I think about the following pages, I am aware that there are many people connected with the on-going development of liturgy who might already have asked some of the questions I discuss: I have tried to keep their questions in a context wide enough to remember the professional choir directors, priests, religious, and members of parish liturgical commissions, as well as those who are doing the folk music — the guitarists and others who make up the groups that help lead us in singing. Some pages are applicable to everyone, some only to those whose experience is new, some to those whose experience is old. Feel free to pick and choose. And if you've heard it before, please go on.

I have tried to remember what I have learned and discussed with others over the years. Together we will pass it on to those who are asking similar questions. I hope our dialogue in these pages will be valuable and enjoyable.

Celebrating With Music

PART
ONE

Blowin' in the Wind . . .

(. . . AS THE SPIRIT WILL !)

December 4, 1963. Dateline: Rome. They promulgated the constitution on the liturgy. We all suddenly got a chance to take part in the liturgy. Wow! We can stand and move around a little. We will actually be interacting with the priest. And with this new involvement we might find that liturgy is something we can get ourselves into (maybe even an emotion or two, if we don't talk about it to too many people). And **singing**.

"I just can't wait to do some of those new songs!"

"Have you heard *Praise to the Lord?*"

"Yeah, and there's a new Kyrie, goes something like dum, de dum dum."

"Sure is nice to be doing things in English. Well, I got to go. Going home to listen to a new hootennanny record."

With Lyre, Harp
and a Flatpick:
The
Folk
Musician
at
Worship

A few months later. . . .

"This new Mass is turning out to be decent. Never knew anything that was going on before; now I know one or two things. Besides it's fun to sing a little. Made me feel a little like when we watch 'Sing Along with Mitch.' "

"You know, last week we had a special service in the hall and since there was no organist someone used a guitar for those neat songs we talked about."

Strum, stee strum strum. . . .

It may not have happened quite so simply but somehow we began to find that there were more ways to accompany music than with the organ. And strangely enough, there were also other types of music to sing besides the long-standing melodies we had sung for so many years. Just what has evolved in the last nine or ten years?

With Lyre, Harp
and a Flatpick:
The
Folk
Musician
at
Worship

Not only have we witnessed new music styles in liturgical worship, but there has been change and development in American music itself. The progressions of new moods and focuses in all the music that is part of our contemporary culture have influenced a vernacular style as well as language in our music for worship.

These years have been times of transition and development in music which few would ever have predicted possible. They exploded out of the energy produced by those first attempts of rock music, which occurred in the mid-50's. Rock had come from the strengths of blues and country music fused together. This new concentration on the beat created places for many new artists to express themselves musically. Some of it was of questionable artistic quality; but, overall, the songs that survived were a reasonable interpretation and expression of the mood of the times.

This mood evolved in the early 60's to one of looking at the society and looking at people. There seemed to be a movement toward simplicity in spite of booming technological advances. With this, musicians were once again conscious of those who had written songs in this mood before. The songs of Woody Guthrie, the Carter Family, Josh White, and other folk singers of this century were resurrected. New songs were written and sung by individuals and groups we are all familiar with: the Kingston Trio, the Brothers Four; and most of all, Peter, Paul, and Mary.

The revival was so powerful that we experienced the hootennanny craze which made everyone and his brother an amateur folk-singer. I become one of the victims of the craze and did a little folk picking myself. I have fond memories of many musical happenings as a result. Surely, you remember times when you first dared to perform in front of a live audience — the mental trauma of wondering how people would like the songs, or worse, if they would like you, the long-rehearsed songs done with friends (who now were a "group"), and all sorts of unplanned versions of songs (which we now professionally call improvisations). I will never forget my first performance. Three of us were doing a set in school. We had rehearsed well, we knew our parts, and each had a well-defined role (namely, "I'll play, you sing"). We got out on the stage and survived the first verse fine. Two lines into the second verse the rhythm fell apart, and someone forgot the words. We were good though. With the ultimate grasp on the situation, I very casually whispered (so that only the first ten rows of people heard it) to my partners, "Keep going or we're dead!" Traumatic, but a start.

**Blowin'
in the Wind . . .**
. . . as
the Spirit will!

About a year later in the cold kitchen of a church in Lancaster, Kentucky, we were sitting around waiting for lunch and some guy had a guitar and said he wanted to teach us a song or two. I remember this incident because I happened to be carrying a spare flat pick in my pocket and this guy didn't have one with him. I felt good helping someone who was then a more experienced musician. We learned a few of these new songs and were surprised to hear that they were intended to be used in church.

19

With Lyre, Harp
and a Flatpick:
The
Folk
Musician
at
Worship

I later came to play with Jack on many occasions and together
we learned a lot about liturgy and helping people sing. We played
those first songs many, many times, until we knew most of them
by heart (and, unfortunately, until people were ready to kill us if
we dared do them again).

Playing those first songs was a big step. We had seen the days
of trying to accompany existing songs on the guitar. That had only
half worked. We also experienced people taking the folk song melodies we were all familiar with and writing new words to them. This
too was only half successful because it was so difficult to disassoci-
ate our experience of the original, and we kept asking questions
like: "If the melody is OK and the song is really speaking what
we want to say, why not use the whole song?" But it would be
years before such things as "secular" music might even get a hearing
for discussion. We now had something that we could really work
with — songs written for the liturgy and for the folk enthusiast,
and maybe this was in line with the new enthusiasm for the liturgy.

The songs first heard in that cold kitchen have lasted a long
time and I am glad they came along when they did. If nothing
else, they were a beginning. We all have seen many songs since
then and we can now choose things which are both musically worthwhile and which speak the things we believe as a Christian community. These last few years have been taken up with trying other things
connected with music. We have combined everything from tambou-
rines and flutes to finger cymbals and glockenspiel.

We have sung songs with all sorts of refrains and repeating
phrases and rounds and impromptu harmonies. We have sung along
with records and heard tapes of the professional entertainers or folk
singers; we have had the chance to clap along with the rhythm, and
with it all we have made progress toward worshipping as a real
Christian family.

The songs have developed considerably as well. There must
have been several thousand songs written in the familiar four chord
pattern and 4/4 time. Some of these have been among the best.
Some, however, we can look at and wonder how we ever dared to
place them in front of the worshipping community.

"I don't know if
we're ready for THAT!"

**Blowin'
in the Wind . . .**
. . . as
the Spirit will!

We have tried to teach songs by various methods ranging from printed song sheets to overhead projectors to the ultimate trust in our people — ESP ("I'm sure they'll know it as soon as they hear it"). Sometimes, we have even taken the time to explain something about the music to them and allow them time to get used to new things; and we have found, as a result, that they all sing rather well if we will be patient enough to let them learn the music.

Sometimes we have put on excellent concerts in church, and people have cheered us for providing the best liturgy they have ever "seen." We have assembled musicians either as soloists or as groups the size of a marching band (and sometimes with equal finesse). We have had them in front so we could see them, even though sometimes as a result we couldn't see the priest. We have put them in choir lofts in the back so no one could either see or hear them. We have avoided spending money for microphones or we have used them in such a way that we would have been better off carpeting the parking lot.

21

With Lyre, Harp
and a Flatpick:
The
Folk
Musician
at
Worship

We have sung off key, not planned, and come too late even to
tune our guitars together. We have taught miserable music, distracted people by our moving around and dropping books, and
done a million other things by which we were able to ruin liturgy.
Still the people of God continue to come back for more. They
stand in crowded places, they come at odd hours, they argue in
sometimes hopeless situations, they draw up petitions, they beg
and plead for us to be able to play for them. And the numbers
are continuing to grow as they hear this "new music."

I list many of these follies about the world of liturgical guitar
picking because they are all real. At least I have seen them **all** and
people of other experience have raised questions in every one of
these areas and more. They too are part of our musical history
along with folk festivals, cold kitchens, and new songs: a process
we are engaged in for bettering our worship and ourselves — thank
the Lord for it all!

Music - a SYMBOL??

Occasionally, we take time to examine whatever got us involved in music, but surely not often enough. What is its attraction and what value does it have? Why did you get into music? What does it do for you? Why bother getting your fingers calloused and sore? Why spend all that time practicing? Surely, it is not to make a living. It probably isn't to invent a new musical form. And I'm sure none of us intends to put the pipe organ builders out of business. There must be some good reason. Why not try to think of some of the reasons? We can do it together. You think of yours, and I'll try to write mine.

I have always been overwhelmed by the mysterious way that things transfer from one person to another with nothing in between them but air being jiggled around. All I have to do is jiggle the air a bit and you get a buzz in your ear — that is, you can hear me. I can tell you hello; I can ask what is inside you; I can bounce something from inside myself off the side of an echoing mountain; I can transfer and let you know part of the rhythm of varied feelings within me. Luckily, we can organize our different vibrations to communicate whatever is our mood or thought or belief, and we can vary them by many subtle changes.

23

With Lyre, Harp
and a Flatpick:
The
Folk
Musician
at
Worship

These movements of air are symbols — they express something of what is inside us. We usually refer to these symbols as sounds. I often have something happening inside myself that I want to express. Very early I learned that moving the air with my voice could express responses to my environment and simple emotions; later I learned that it could communicate more complex feelings, as well as abstract ideas, whole ranges of thought. And later still I found that various other things moved the air — pianos, horns, cymbals, and strings — and that these sound-producers in someone else's hands were able to let me know a great deal of what was going on inside that person.

These sounds generally had an influence on my mood, an influence which could sometimes be drastic. Strange things would happen: sometimes my foot would begin to move in vibrations similar to the instrument's, my fingers might begin tapping with some enthusiasm, or I might just begin to feel different because of the sounds. I have experienced musical phenomena that have caused large crowds of people to respond by moving their whole bodies in dancing or by clapping along with it.

Possibly the most profound thing which goes on with those mysterious uses of sounds is what happens when many people are together and move the air with the same vibrations. They are, by their presence together, and their expression together, able to generate the energy of common cause, or belief, or faith. The first time I sang *Lights of the City* was in Evansville, Indiana. About five hundred people came to a concert at the end of a worship. As a bridge between my set and Erich Sylvester's, we did the song together. The power with which the people sang was overwhelming. We knew that we were right together as we sang the song — "I can almost see the lights of the city, forever Lord I shall be free." What we experience at that point is a symbol of great strength. We experience the reality of what is happening within each one of the persons gathered together. We know it because of the expression it is given.

We now have something of a tool to uncover how we share the oneness known as the people of God. These regulated sounds and words are what we so casually call music — they are our songs.

I have found that there is much to be gained from having this symbol or tool at my fingertips. Many things can happen. I can add something extra — more life, more zip — to my expression of what I see going on around me. Also, I can capture something I am not personally able to express by using another person's symbols. When I want to say something which is not quite clear in my own mind, or is difficult to express, very often I can find a song written by someone of similar experience. This helps in two ways. First, it is a way of saying what I intend to say, and then it is a share in the experience and accompanying insight of whoever wrote the song. With these aids it is possible to call to mind, at any time, some of the thought or feeling attached to significant events. This can prove both healthy and enjoyable. Repeating songs gives us a chance to revitalize or at least continue to some degree these significant events. They serve as reminders and reinforcers of what we believe.

They also get the air moving just right between people so that there is not only a vibration of molecules but also a passage of the most positive form of energy — the love for one another and its accompanying care for one another that is the message of the Gospel. Song regenerates our consciousness of what we Christians have: a freedom from darkness and slavery . . . a call to be the simple who will confuse the wise . . . and a faith that will help us be willing to say what we believe . . . out loud!

There are more reasons for my interest in music, but I will save them for a while. If your experience is anything like mine has been, you have found that during the times when you are not so sure why you keep playing, the playing is not really that good anyway. Recalling those times, I know that I have had to answer that question before I could hope to perform in front of anyone.

25

We don't often use the word <u>symbol</u> to describe music because it is next to impossible to have a clear notion of symbol. It could be that we are just not paying attention to what happens when we use symbols, or more emphatically, what happens if we cease to use them. We know that there is only so much of ourselves we can communicate to one another, and the only way we can is by using some sort of a tool. If we have clear symbols, we communicate well. Obscure symbols obscure expression and hence either hinder our communication or prevent it.

My experience has been that there are few places where this is more true and applicable than in the celebration of liturgy. The liturgical use of symbols is analogous to serious interpersonal relationships: If a person does not say things properly, he either does not know what is going on with the other person, or worse, they drift apart because of the resulting confusion. Unfortunately, this seems to happen often within our Christian community. Either the symbols themselves are unclear, or worse, their misuse hinders understanding. Frustration results and people gradually come to say that there is no reason to be there, nothing is happening. And nothing *is* happening for them. They are not receiving anything of the reality communicated symbolically for one simple reason — the symbol is not speaking to them. This is not always the fault of the symbol, but sometimes the fault of the symbol maker. Without trying to analyze all the symbols of the liturgy, we will look at the part we are involved with as guitar pickers — music.

When we sing, we are in a position to take something from the composer, if we give his art work an opportunity to touch us. Here, perhaps, lies the key to music. When music touches us, there is a symbolic exchange, for something of the writer's or performer's experience is open to us. The artist knows something from what he has lived. He puts it in a medium. He makes a symbol of it and presents it to us. If we decide to hear it, if we let the symbol come within ourselves, we can then understand and

With Lyre, Harp
and a Flatpick:
The
Folk
Musician
at
Worship

possibly relate very closely to the artist's experience. Play your
favorite song and notice what is happening. Our fantasy is very
active when we hear a story and feel its mood. What is it that
makes the song come alive? I am sure it is not the words alone!
Somewhere within the melody and the rhythm, the story bears
a mysterious power to capture the imagination.

A freeing takes place in the experiencing of music, a freeing
of our emotions. We can legitimately feel something. It is per-
fectly all right to laugh or cry because of a song. Here is one of
the few occasions when our emotions are "socially acceptable."

Men have recognized a strange power in music and have made
music for as long as we can remember. The Bible refers to it from
the earliest chapters of Genesis which name Jubal as the father of
all those who play the lyre and pipe. In 1 Samuel 16, we read,
"Saul said, 'Let David remain in my service, for he has found favor
in my sight.' And whenever the evil spirit from God was upon
Saul, David took the lyre and played it with his hand; so Saul was
refreshed and the evil spirit departed from him." Among my favorite passages is Colossians 3:14, "And above all put on love which
binds all in perfect harmony. And let the peace of Christ rule in
your hearts and be thankful. Let the word of Christ dwell in you
richly as you teach and admonish one another with all wisdom and
as you sing songs and hymns and spiritual songs with thankfulness
in your hearts." It is probably no accident that those verses use
harmony, oneness, peace, and *songs*; they seem to point out much
of the spiritual nature of music. It is more than just sounds and
words; it causes common vibration with the very core of our being.
We gain something when the total self is, as it were, vibrating in
harmony. Our experience attains a wholeness. Therefore, music
as symbol points to a wholeness we have as well as a wholeness
we continue to work for. It allows us to reach a depth not readily
available at all times.

This is appropriate when we move to the realm of liturgical
celebration. We want our oneness to be expressed, but need help
throughout our celebrations to remind us that there is something
of a unity within our Christian community. The bishops remarked
in their document, *Music in Catholic Worship,* that "if a sign needs

explanation to communicate faith they will often be watched instead of celebrated." The effectiveness of music is so close to our nature that when we are together in song nothing needs to be explained. Song allows more of our faith to be realized. It helps in the times when we do not feel like being celebrative. It brings vitality to what we believe. Most of all, in its vagueness, it allows us, indeed invites us, to put our unique existential situation together with many others, into one of harmonic similarity without tampering with individuality. This harmony reflects something of the presence of God, mysteriously.

The more technical aspects of performing liturgical music, which we are ready to examine, will make most sense if we have a clear perspective of what we hope to do. We should therefore refresh our thinking about **what** we are celebrating.

We have all grown up knowing there is a strong connection between worship and what we have experienced as our religious upbringing. Regularly, we have gone to church and seen and perhaps even participated in liturgy. Unfortunately, one question is repeated over and over again: "What is going on?" By citing several related topics, I can give something of an answer.

29

To begin with, worship has to do with us as Christian people. Being a Christian is being part of a group of people who have somehow heard the message of Jesus. Faith may be seen as a **response** to hearing this Word. We hear the message, and because it makes sense to us and we are invited to this community of believers, we respond: we **do** something which lets others know we are hearing the message.

This "doing" may take many forms: the way we live, the way we relate to our neighbor, or the way we speak. It also should include the way we are willing to admit our response to God with others who have heard the Word. One kind of response is joining in common prayer. This is a public action which states we are believers and are united, or are at least working toward being united to other believers. Liturgy, then, is a way members of a community pray together; and this prayer is one of thanks for the relationship which exists between God and man.

We offer praise to God for many things: creation, friends, family, to name but a few. God has done things for us and by these things has told us much about who He is. His greatest telling came in the person of Jesus, who in His life and message of many paradoxes lets us know that love is possible in spite of us. He also told us that this love is powerful enough to bring us to the kingdom of God.

Jesus used a method of praising His Father common to all Jews in His day — the Passover meal. The Jewish people celebrated their deliverance from Egypt in this special meal. They **remembered** how God had helped them when they were in slavery. Jesus knew this, and besides recalling the feast of Passover, gave us a way of remembering what he was to do for us: die and rise for us. We now get together for some of these reasons. We are remembering and acknowledging our gratitude for the good things God has done for us; and we are by a special set of actions carrying on what Jesus told us to do as a Christian community. In doing so we remind ourselves of our freedom, responsibility, hope and unity. Finally, because we have not reached perfection in all of these, we also strengthen each other in our movement toward becoming a true believing community able to share a meal in peace looking for the coming of the Lord.

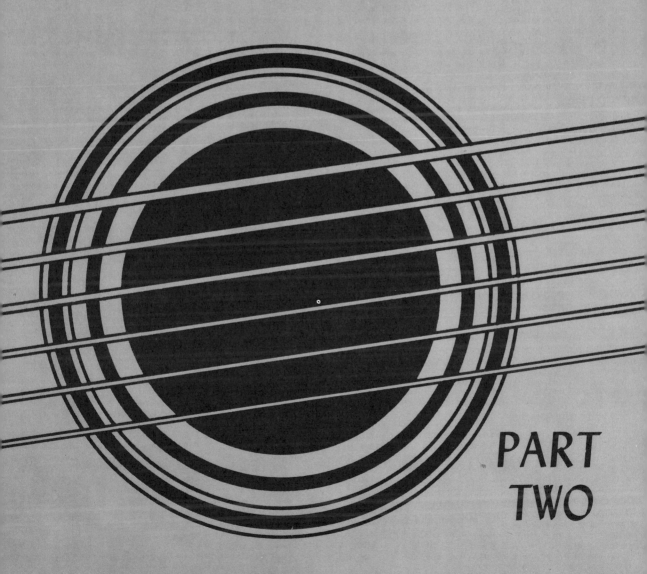

Leading the Congregation

PART TWO

INTRODUCTION TO PART TWO

This next section will deal with the essentials of leading the congregation in singing. When we say that we will lead the singing in our parishes, we are volunteering to take part in the most powerful human resource available to the people of God. No slight task. It does not seem too much to ask that we find some way to remain very aware of this when we are preparing or actually leading singing. We commonly reassure ourselves by thinking of how much we enjoy leading the singing or by remembering comments from the congregation that they "get a lot out of it." These thoughts keep us knowing that we are helping people worship. A complete perspective, however, reminds us that if we rely only on these reassurances or presume people will come no matter how we play, we invite disaster. I believe that every celebration deserves to be considered "the first" in order to reflect the unique gathering it actually is. By approaching each celebration as unique, we challenge the best in ourselves as leaders and musicians; and we keep before ourselves the knowledge that we are helping the people in the most important part of their spiritual lives: the praising of God.

In a nutshell, people are counting on us to help them in an area so mysterious and profound, yet so important to them that they will do a great deal to make it work. People want to worship; they know it has an important connection to the way they live; and they are grateful for whatever we can do to bring life and worship together.

1

Relationship

A. GETTING TO KNOW THE CONGREGATION

John tells of a city, so high up above
Where we'll meet in a spirit of love;
We'll meet over yonder, in that heavenly place
There we'll see each other face to face.

This first verse of a recent song I learned gives me a chance to think about what is involved when we are spending any time together with a group of people.

At a recent evening meal at the community to which I belong we were discussing various Epistles. I was very struck by the words of John when he was closing his second and third epistles and said that although he had much to write he would rather "come to see you to talk face to face so that our joy may be complete" (1 John 12). Later that evening I was at the Family Owl, a local coffeehouse,

With Lyre, Harp
and a Flatpick:
The
Folk
Musician
at
Worship

listening to a new arrival from New Orleans. Ron Sowell ended his evening performance with the song about John's desire of seeing each other face to face. Its clarity kept reminding me about the whole matter of really meeting people; of how when we really speak to one another we look at one another; and how this can result in knowing more about each other.

Although our relationship with the congregation is not quite the same as that with intimate friends, it is definitely of a personal nature and can only be accomplished when we take the time to meet the people. I often recall the feeling of being invited to someone's house for an evening or for dinner. Many times there would be some other guests I did not know. We would usually struggle through assorted topics of discussion ranging from the length of the lawn to important social issues like when the new lines would be painted on the street. Really a tremendous time! If, however, we were together for some purpose, or if we bothered to find out something about each other, a much more important exchange took place. We could often find out that there was a commonality of values.

When gathering in the name of the Lord, there are similar things occurring. There is commonality in our moving as the people of God, and by accomplishing some unity that pilgrimage is able to go forward. We can, as leaders of song, do a great deal to let this be realized if we will begin by meeting the congregation and taking the time to let them know more of our purpose rather than simply announcing that "we will sing number 27 for the first song."

In spite of the fact that many people are accustomed to someone being active on the altar either as celebrant, lector, song leader, or server, there is room to have activities made clearer. It is important for us as leaders to be confortable with the congregation so that they can become confortable with us. Then we can all express our faith as it is, rather than with great strain and reluctance. Although there is a risk involved in expressing belief in a person, or understanding or love, there is no reason for it to be a painful experience. The celebration of love is an experience of man's most joyous

moments, notwithstanding the struggle, tension and risk involved in loving another. When the other is God, there should be no exception made. Surely, struggle, tension and risk are present in this love relationship — all the more because of our difficulty in understanding. Nevertheless, we do experience His presence in our assembled community, we know something of His message, and we experience His presence in the Word. It is by way of our successfully leading the people in the celebration that our experience of Him is most effectively brought about. So, as we work toward making symbols operative, we start by being able to work well with the congregation, meeting them as individuals and as elements of a community. This meeting gives us a setting in which we can all learn from one another, and can effectively speak our faith as members of the church. It cannot be made too clear — we are hardly able to be anything of a community if we have no idea who the other members are.

39

B. **HOW TO GET
    THEM TO SING** —
    *(" YOU WILL
    SING UND YOU
    VILL LIKE IT!")*

One of our favorite song-leader types was recently recorded as he introduced a new song to his congregation:

"Now that we have you gathered here to praise the Lord we will proceed to make your response of faith such that it is the best way possible and so that it is genuine and so that you sing with gusto, and that we all sing together, in perfect harmony and rhythm and believe strongly and are a community with the same faith and we will from now on enjoy our celebrations immensely every time we get together, because this is the best way to do it and should last a long time. So take your books and we will sing heartily number 83 . . . ."

As I reflect on the folk tradition, one of the strongest themes of the songs written over the years is that of freedom and removal of oppression in order to find individual ways to live. This has carried over to our liturgy as we struggle to have the chance to use forms which were not outlined in the *Didache,* or some other ancient document. Or maybe we struggle to restore some ancient part or emphasis which we see should remain in celebrations of our Christianity.

These aspects of the folk tradition, when kept in our awareness, will give some beginnings of an answer to the question which has been asked more than any other: **How do you get people to sing?** This question is like the search for the grail among liturgical musicians; they are haunted by it and will not rest until they find some solution.

The best resolution of that search has come to me only lately. **YOU DON'T!!** But before you throw the book away, hold on a minute. Think for a moment; what are we asking by wanting to get people to sing? We are saying something about having the best way for each person in that church at that time, much like our leader-type we heard from above. Are we sure at any given time that our offering of songs is even close to what certain people need, want, or will benefit by?

This does not negate our work and preparation for a celebration; nor does it deny our leadership as being of utmost importance. It says our best hope is to have people accept our **invitation** to sing. My experience has been that this is the approach which makes all the difference. You will recall the notion of meeting the congregation. When we have an accepting relationship with another person, we allow ourselves to be content with his difference. We are usually happy with uniqueness. When we are really open to another, we can accept conclusions which are not the same as our own. They do not threaten us.

If we can be that open with a congregation, very likely they will respond to it. In a word, we will then be *helping* them celebrate rather than *telling* them to celebrate. We should *invite* the

41

With Lyre, Harp
and a Flatpick:
The
Folk
Musician
at
Worship

congregation to sing, both through a simple and open request to do so and and by doing the music very well. Our doing a good job is an implicit but powerful invitation! Consider that those who come to the mass come more or less freely; something encourages them to be there. Probably the type of music and the type of celebration speak to their faith, so we already have a start. Beyond this "given," however, there is much to understand about the liturgy and about the best way for involving the congregation.

The scholars and people who write guidelines and documents and synods are trying to help. As unique as we all are, we realize many similarities. As Christian people, we do want to express our faith, or we want somehow to be able to pray. The help we need is to be able to do so. To give this help is the main responsibility of the leader of song. Only when we are in harmony with the belief and the needs of the individuals of the congregation will they have any desire to sing; and until they want to sing, don't waste your energy or worry about trying to force them. The strange paradox is that when we leave people be and at the same time are able to have concern for them and are interested in their being able to celebrate the Lord, they are often right with us.

Are we therefore interested enough in our people that we can remember that on any given day several might not feel like singing, many might have sore throats, many might have small children with them who require attention, some might never have heard the song, a few might not like that particular one, we might be doing it poorly, they might not be able to hear us, they might not understand what the song is about, or they might be thinking about what it is saying, they might be thinking about the last song we sang, or a thousand other things? If all these mental events were happening simultaneously, we might be singing a solo, but it could result in a very important faith experience for all the people in the church, except the musicians who would be considering themselves total failures.

Joe Wise, popular folk composer and gentle master of the art of inviting people to sing.

With Lyre, Harp
and a Flatpick:
The
Folk
Musician
at
Worship

This is an extreme example, I know, but I want to strongly remind all of you who are trying so hard to increase the participation in your churches: we will do the best job of encouraging singing if we are well prepared and are close to what is going on in the congregation — and in the end are able to communicate this to the people. A genuine invitation is another way of our contributing to the church's being a group of believers who respect one another and who are able to **choose** their own best way of praising God. We need to be clear about this choosing and we need to let everyone know we acknowledge it. Music done properly will be its own invitation; people seeing our belief as we sing will be able to relate this to their particular place and experience.

As encouraging as this might sound, there is a tension which comes to mind. Are we saying to wait around until everyone conforms to our wishes? Are we saying that we don't care about those who are not singing? Neither! We are saying that we want to share our faith with those who have gathered and we hope our choices are helpful to them. It is in a vague area and difficult to explain, for it is not in the realm of technical preparations for leading singing. The technical aspects are important and we will discuss many; however, the bond of the Christian family is much more mysterious than good knots tied in microphone wire, and its expression more profound than volume levels and rhythm.

I have great confidence that the more you think about what you are doing as you celebrate with the people by leading the singing, and the more you are willing to be in an open and accepting relationship with them, the more they will be eager to respond and sing out the faith that they hold so deeply inside themselves. As you combine radiating your own belief with perfecting certain techniques which make for clarity and support of the congregation, you may begin to find the whole parish group moving towards experiencing some of the care for one another which John's Gospel describes so often.

C. RESPECTING THE CONGREGATION; CRITICISM — VARIOUS RESPONSES

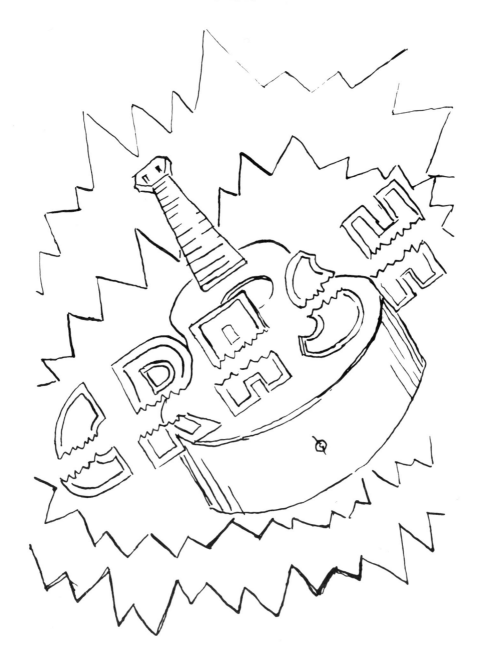

With Lyre, Harp
and a Flatpick:
The
Folk
Musician
at
Worship

Among our invitations to the congregation, we must add one of opening ourselves to the most helpful, but often most painful, part of dialogue — criticism. We need to make it very clear that we wish to know what the congregation thinks of the planning, execution, and overall value of the music we are offering them.

Most of our association with criticism, unfortunately, has been in negative terms and, therefore, as something to be feared and avoided. Openness to criticism in the realm of music, on the other hand, can become one of our most valuable ways of expanding our skills and therefore better serving the people of God. There is no easy way that I have found to remove that fear, but I am sure it is better to know the things which hinder people's singing, or which generally annoy them, rather than have them quit coming to church on Sunday. If we listen to criticism, we will be attempting to accomodate everyone who comes to the service.

There are several types of criticism we are likely to receive, and they range from excited praise to raving condemnation. These extremes sometimes cancel one another out, but it is the shades of appreciation and opinion which we must search out from the people of the parish. We can gain this information in a variety of ways including printed surveys, phone call inquiries and letters: these are helpful, but they demand time and money. During the periods between major surveying, a very effective method is to concentrate on talking to several people at the end of every service or liturgy. If you see new people each time you play and ask them one or two questions about the day's music, you are certain to get helpful comments.

As for your questions, you must ask them in such a way as to invite authentic comments. And be specific: Find out responses to the new song of the day, or ask —

> if a certain key was comfortable, or
>> if you should keep a certain song, or
>>> if the song in question was easy to learn, or
>>>> if the words could be understood, or
>>>>> if the congregation knew when to come in. . . .

If this information is remembered and recorded, you will gain a running commentary on the music in your parish. And you might end up making a new friend or two as the weeks go by and you see many new people. Another possibility for eliciting criticism is to meet a few people before the liturgy begins and ask them to pay special attention to the way things go on that day; then discuss the service with them afterwards. You will find this kind of involvement of people in the service contributes markedly to the development of the parish.

There are many specifics which should be considered in the overall criticism of choosing, playing, and leading music. There will be further and detailed examples and aids in a later chapter, so you need not think this is all there is to criticism. It is an on-going and demanding process which must be as important as knowing the congregation and planning to lead the music properly.

2

The Performers

A. REHEARSALS —
UNTIL YOU CAN DO IT IN YOUR SLEEP!

There comes a time in our experience as musicians that some of the patterns and techniques which we so painfully learned are second nature (I'll bet you thought you'd arrived when you did your first F chord). This seems to be the only consolation for the difficulty and innate reluctance to work on a new song or a new picking style or new chords or things as disgusting as scales.

I have tried and tried but still have not come up with a secret potion to pour on your fingers or a magic formula for getting one hand to be synchronized with the other. It sounds terribly traditional and perhaps outdated to bring up such ancient encouragements as *Repetitio est mater studiorum* (repetition is the mother of learning), but there seems to be truth in the axiom. I guess we must say something like *Repetitio est mater pickiorum.*

In any case, the pleasure of doing a new lick, or being able to really move with the flow of a song is something we arrive at only when we have taken the time to conquer the technical or muscular or coordinating part of the song; hence we come to a

With Lyre, Harp
and a Flatpick:
The
Folk
Musician
at
Worship

discussion of such a topic as **Rehearsal**, and offer the suggestion that you be able to play the music and move about in front of the congregation almost without thinking about what you are doing.

I have a theory which says, "When you know something well enough that you don't have to think about it, then you can think about it." When I am playing a song or leading a group, many things are going on — chords, words, rhythm, melody, runs, listening, etc. When a song is done well, all these things are done in harmony. Surprisingly, even though they are going on together,

none is done without at least some attention. Notice the next time you do a song. You may find yourself knowing that it is time to change to a new chord, you know what kind of rhythm you are doing with your right hand, you think about hammering-on for a new note, and for sure you know when you miss on any of these.

50

When we play with this kind of attention, we are continually moving back and forth between being technicians and being artists. Mechanical actions become creative. When we master the technical aspects of a song, we are then, and only then, able to work towards a level of music as art — one of communication, feeling and symbol. It is, therefore, very important to take care of this kind of preparation if we intend for the music to be complete. And there is no doubt in my mind that this *is* attainable by any one of you who knows more than two chords— if you are willing to take some time for it. Part III of this book offers you the opportunity to learn a number of new 'licks.' Would you be willing to learn two or three of them now and one new one each week for the next six months? They are all variations and additions to basic chords that we all learned once upon a time, and they are clearly in context of the kinds of songs we are used to singing with our congregations.

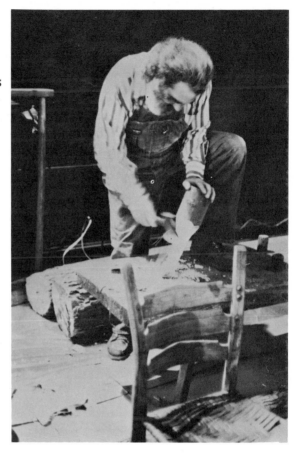

When some of these are learned, they help the congregation to understand or experience the songs — but only if integrated into the music. For example, a three-note run might be just right to help people know when to come in for a refrain, but if the group all but stops to get set for those notes and then makes them stand out drastically, the subtle help then becomes a distracting jar to the flow of the music. Rather than helping the congregation better

With Lyre, Harp
and a Flatpick:
The
Folk
Musician
at
Worship

express their faith, we have kept them from thinking about anything but the structure of the song and the heavy-handedness of
the song leaders (who at that point are probably paying so much
attention to those three notes that they will lose their place in
the words of the song).

When you are rehearsing a song, you might remember a few
things. Talk over what your group thinks of the song, its meaning,
mood, style, and anything else related to how you will interpret it.
Try to come to a decision which you agree on, and then STICK
WITH IT! Consistency is very important when you rehearse; without it, you will not know what to expect the next time you do
the song, nor will you be able to become familiar with the way it
will be done. Rehearse the version, dividing up if necessary to
accomplish smoothness; do it a few times noticing the rough spots.
When reasonably together, go over it one more time to be sure.

You want to gain confidence in your playing I am sure: a
few good renditions of a song will help immensely. As you gain
confidence with the song, work toward giving attention to dynamics
of volume and pace. They help emphasize important parts of the
song. Write these in the music if it will help. Finally, check to be
sure each member is OK with what he is doing while others are
playing. Know that you have a solid arrangement and definite
parts, smooth it out, and you're ready to go on Sunday.

B. ROLES WITHIN
THE GROUP OF MUSICIANS

Once your group has learned the basics of singing together you may find there is now room for development. When a group is new, all efforts are spent on performing together with consistency. We usually do our best to support one another in those traumatic early days of playing in front of people. We have simple arrangements and sing together in order that the overall goal may be accomplished — people will hear what we are singing.

But we should remember that after the group reaches its optimum size there is no longer good reason for everyone to do exactly the same thing. Each member has a role. If we keep this in mind, we can create better arrangements. We must take care of the main priorities of leading with clearly understood singing and consistent, helpful accompaniment. Because of the nature of different songs, it is often necessary to divide these priorities among the members of the group. Some songs are difficult to sing and, therefore, should be arranged with one person singing and others concentrating on accompaniment. If everyone is able to sing, attention should be given to making the accompaniment better musically by way of variations or instrumentation such as mentioned in the Appendix.

We should know what each member does best whether it be singing lead or harmony or not singing at all, whether it be playing a picking pattern or strumming or playing bass runs. With this knowledge of each group member's strengths, you will be better able to plan good arrangements and thus eliminate forcing one person to do everything. Above all, be willing to recognize difficulties and to make adjustments so that the priorities mentioned will come through clearly. As much as we like playing, we will be much more helpful if, on occasion, one or more persons lets the guitar sit for a given song in order for the words to be done well. In this way, we again contribute to letting the congregation know our interest in their being able to sing well.

53

With Lyre, Harp
and a Flatpick:
The
Folk
Musician
at
Worship

C. HOW DO YOU FEEL
ABOUT YOUR PLAYING?

I have been lucky to spend time playing music with many people throughout the country. They have taught me the things I know as a musician. Among us all, however, we have never been able to work successfully with the question of confidence as musicians. I have often been very impressed with the talent of the people I have met but surprised to find that some refuse to play, or that they play only with great reluctance. They are not sure how the music will be received and do not wish to take a chance that it will not be appreciated. This reluctance is part of an even wider question that we all wrestle with. Few of us are eager to perform in any way in front of large groups because we are never sure how our efforts will be received.

It would be remarkable if there were a rational or logical method for letting someone know that his music is of good quality and that we are eager to hear it. Reason, however, generally fails us in this discussion. It is only when we experience acceptance of our performance that we will actually trust the encouraging remarks that have been made to us. When you feel that your music is lacking something or you fear that your playing is not what it should be, I encourage you to discuss your feelings with other musician friends. If others hear you and you are able to discuss some of your reluctance, you may progress in gaining confidence. No matter what is said and no matter what the encouragements are, in the end gaining confidence always seems to come from trial by fire. We are continually faced with doubt about playing music. I encourage you to stay with it. I cannot tell you how to feel better about your playing but my experience has been that everyone who is willing to play in church and who attempts to lead singing has much to offer. This offering includes not only musical talent but also personal willingness to contribute something for the good of the parish family.

If we allow ourselves to be hindered every time we hear some-one who plays or sings better than we do, we will slow the process of becoming better musicians. We can find hope in watching others who play better than we do, particularly if we remember that they, at one time, knew only as much as we do. If we are interested in developing as musicians and song leaders, we need to have people whose experience encourages us to learn more. The desire to play like your favorite musicians should give you patience during the slow and sometimes imperceptible progressions from one level of expertise to another.

One other way of encouraging yourself is to keep a log of the things you learn. If you decide to learn one new skill a week or every other week, you may be surprised at the development which takes place over a short space of a few months. By learning new skills and practicing them regularly, you will quickly grow both more comfortable and more confident with the music. As this happens, you will be better able to meet the congregation and they to meet you; as a result, you will receive more encouragement from them and your self-assurance will continue to grow.

3

Right Before the Start

A. TEACHING NEW SONGS

*"Can't say much about teaching,
but I am very interested in learning . . ."*

These words of wisdom from the noted psychologist-educator
Carl Rogers give us another insight into our role of leading music
in celebrations. It doesn't make much difference how well we
teach people if we do not make it possible for them to learn.
Sound strange?

As we think seriously about helping our congregations, we are
more aware that it is our moving toward their need that makes for
the best progress. The area of learning new songs is no exception.
A person is best able to sing a song when he knows the words, is
familiar with the rhythm, can count on the speed, and is asked to
sing in a key which fits his own range. Usually, when these conditions are available, all we have to do is present a good song to
people and they will be right along with us as we sing.

With Lyre, Harp
and a Flatpick:
The
Folk
Musician
at
Worship

It is our task to create those conditions which encourage and enable the congregation in singing. When teaching a song, it is most important to have the people know the words — they get rather discouraged if they have to mumble along as so often happens with prayers that everyone is supposed to know by heart. Most folks would just as soon not bother singing along with us if they are forced to stumble constantly. OK? Let them learn the words. There are assorted ways to take care of this.

A brief word on these "assorted ways" is in order here. It IS possible for hymns and songs to be learned "by rote", if you are patient and have excellent diction and ennunciation. However, we all know that some kind of printed edition of the songs, offering at least the words, is highly desirable. While a number of different song books, several hymnals, and a variety of "missalettes" are on the market, we've all experienced the repeated frustration of no one publication containing enough of the "right" songs for our celebration. Exactly what congregational participation materials we use is something we musicians are constantly tossing around with the liturgy committees and pastors with whom we work. The most practical alternative for our folk songs in this era of transition and development is ye faithful mimeographed sheet or song folder.

Several matters are of great importance in preparing special songsheets or booklets for your congregation:

1. Get the help and talent necessary to make the printed sheets neat and attractive. Smears and typos not only detract from the celebration itself, but they can be a serious distraction to the people trying to sing from them.

2. If the songs are copyrighted by a publisher or individual composer, obtain written permission to reprint them, even if you are only typing out the texts. Most songs we tend to want to use ARE indeed copyrighted, and most publishers DO have procedures established to assist you in having permission to reprint them legally. The small royalties charged compensate not only the publisher but rewards and encourages the composer as well.

"It's on the house, brother. We didn't pay nuthin' for it."

*We musicians should be the first to encourage
these proper procedures and should consistently advise
against the rationalization in the name of religion which
we know takes place. Our efforts here can help generate
respect and appreciation for the worth of liturgical music
and its musicians, you and me.*

However you do it, give a chance for the words to have their
effect. Music has a power about it, but if the words become distracting because they cannot be understood, something will surely
be lost. Sometimes it is worthwhile to recite them even if the
people have the words in front of them: as an introduction to
what the rhythm of their recitation will be. For the most part,
the average song can be taught in about three tries, or three tries
per section when the refrain is particularly long.

As soon as you have sung it once for the people (offering
them a chance to hum along), invite them to give it a try, and
immediately begin listening to how they are doing. Many songs
have a measure or single note which will deserve extra attention —

With Lyre, Harp
and a Flatpick:
The
Folk
Musician
at
Worship

sometimes the part which makes a song distinctive and a little better than average — and you should be willing to point this section out to the congregation so that they do not round off a nice edge someone may have worked hard to build into a song. You must also listen to know if the song has been put into the right key, although attention to the key of the song is best thought about during rehearsal. If the key needs to be changed and movement of the capo will fix it, don't hesitate to do so. (Unless you are very comfortable with transposing, I wouldn't recommend changing keys on the spot.)

The people may now be singing weakly with you, but nonetheless, giving it a good try. You may bring out melody sometimes by doing it once a capello and using your hand to demonstrate the ups and downs of the melody. This really lets the people know you are trying to help them learn the song and it may add to the gaining of confidence which they need to sing out with gusto.

If you are not pressed for time, usually when teaching only one song, it is advisable to do one verse of the song, so they will know how they are to come in when it is their turn. This is also a chance for them to become comfortable with the real speed of a song. When all this has been done and you want to use up the rest of your two or three minutes, ask a question or two to find out how comfortable the congregation is at this point with the song.

There may be rare occasions when it is good to wait on a song rather than have it really flop. It will not happen often, but don't exclude it completely from the realm of possibility. In any case, try to find out if people really can sing the song. If they do well, a word of encouragement or compliment is very worthwhile.

There is one last phase of teaching which we rarely consider and it is that of secondary teaching. This takes place during the actual singing of the song or on a later day. When doing a relatively new song, remember to give the people a chance to be refreshed or to review the new refrain or verse by repeating it when possible. When you do this, it reminds them that they did learn it at one time and need only to pick it up again. All these suggestions are ways in which we renew our idea of helping people **learn** songs and therefore be better able to celebrate with us as we sing.

B. HOW MUCH
CAN PEOPLE LEARN AT A TIME ?

It depends on the *congregation* and the *occasion.*

Each congregation is unique in both ability and enthusiasm. As leaders we wish to call them to as much as they can be, yet respecting how they are. (cf. "The Gentle Challenge", p. 101). The most general goals seem to be to keep learning, but give time to really learn — and to neither overburden nor underestimate a group. If we are with a group regularly, we can teach with a long range plan — and possibly a more gradual pace. If it is the only time we will be together, it may be necessary to cover more ground in hope of a lasting effect.

A group may be very new to folk music — or to singing — and we must take care not to overburden. Others may be quite comfortable learning a new song frequently. Do not presume without foundation, however — ask them!

The occasion is the other important factor in deciding how much to teach. There have been times when a very enthusiastic group has been able to learn as many as six refrains and sing them well during the celebration. This type of success is usually possible, however, only on very special occasions such as weddings, baptisms or ordinations, where we know that people have **chosen** to be there and are pratically eager to celebrate. Retreats or workshops are another example (slightly different, however, because the learning may be spread out over a day or done at a leisurely pace as the liturgy is being prepared). These times do differ from the average Sunday liturgy which is at least slightly pressured by the clock.

In short, we may say that people CAN learn a great deal, and we will often be surprised by their ability. On special days we can take a chance on teaching more than usual.

With Lyre, Harp
and a Flatpick:
The
Folk
Musician
at
Worship

C. THE PITFALLS
OF ROUTINE REHEARSALS BEFORE MASS

"Hey, will you hurry up, we're going to be late again!"

"Why worry? They practice for hours, we have plenty of time, and we'll still get there before mass begins."

* * *

Later: *". . . and for the seventh song today, we'll do another new one. There are only eight lines for you to memorize so it won't be any trouble. . . ."*

So far, I have taken for granted the importance of the pre-mass warm-up, or music rehearsal, but perhaps a word or two on its use and occasional misuse will now be in order.

Ever wonder about when to start? Masses are scheduled close together and, if people cannot get out of the parking lot for others to get in, there will be chaos. Much of it is likely to land squarely on your head as music leader if you are to blame for overly long practices. Heaven forbid that we should have to base our liturgy on how long it takes people to clear out before the next mass, but there is something to be said for promptness.

We must be ready to go ON TIME! Rehearsing music is among the really difficult parts of our whole task, whether it be with the group alone, or with the congregation (c.f., *Until You Can Do It in Your Sleep*). Because of the difficult nature of rehearsing, we must do everything we can to make it a worthwhile experience for the congregation. This includes several things:

□ **beginning promptly**   □ **making it personal**

□ **proceeding with directness**   □ **keeping it brief**

If you have been leading the congregation for a long time, they may not be used to rehearsing regularly. I suspect that you will have used other methods for teaching, such as singing a second communion song or meditation song which the people will eventually learn, or singing a song while people are coming in. These methods are workable but, in terms of our relationship to the congregation, we should take the time to re-establish contact each week. Variety in rehearsal will keep the congregation alert. If they know beforehand that we will always practice three or four songs, they are likely to begin coming late. If, on the other hand, we only practice one or two songs some weeks and spend the time other weeks explaining songs, this period may prove to be very worthwhile for all in terms of singing, learning about liturgy, and being able to grow as a community.

I am aware that many of you are reluctant to introduce rehearsal times on a regular basis. People I have talked with express reasons such as "the parish won't like it" or "we're afraid to do it." In either case I would suggest that you work towards some introductory time before the service begins. You may find this is not only helpful for the singing but will give assistance to you and the other musicians in gaining confidence as leaders.

With Lyre, Harp
and a Flatpick:
The
Folk
Musician
at
Worship

Much of the reasoning for regular rehearsal is very similar to our discussion on meeting the congregation. If we are to increase our trust in each other and our sense of community, we must be willing to work together in those few minutes immediately before the beginning of worship. By our patient encouragement and careful listening, the congregation will know of our interest in them. Don't forget to thank them for their attentiveness as they have learned.

4

The Technicalities

of Praying Together in Song

A. GOOD LITURGY — GOOD PERFORMANCE:
A CLASH ???

Once upon a time we gave a concert in church. But we never really intended to do that: we thought we were leading the singing at a celebration of the liturgy. I found that it was a concert, though, because of the remarks people made after it.

Once upon a time I went to a liturgy at our concert hall here in the city. I thought it was to be a concert, but it turned out that everyone was really together singing with the performers: it became a celebration.

It is so hard to tell the difference sometimes. How good is too good for the parish, when are we performing, and when are we leading? Is there much need for a difference? The bishops' statement on music and the liturgy says that there is no place for performances or virtuousity for its own sake in the liturgy. Then we shouldn't play too well all the time?

With Lyre, Harp
and a Flatpick:
The
Folk
Musician
at
Worship

There has often been occasion for criticism of leaders of music over the years: they are putting on a show, or they are too good for the congregation. The criticism is a very valid one, but need not frighten us — or relieve us of the responsibility of improving

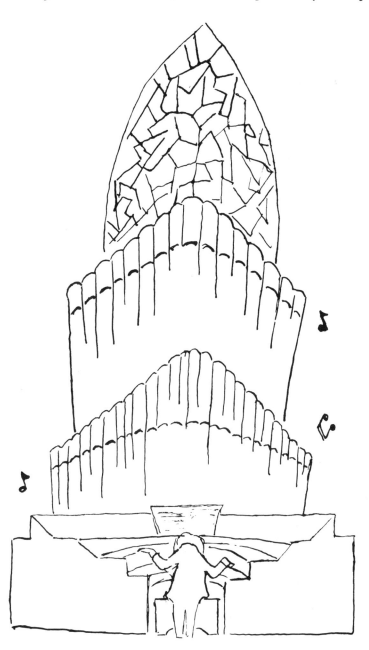

as musicians. It should be seen as a response to a real need — people come to celebrate and pray, not to see a show! The distinction which helps us is to know when we are doing something **for** the congregation as opposed to doing something **with** the congregation. As long as we are able to say honestly that we are working toward leading the celebration, we are usually doing the right thing. When, however, we leave the congregation behind, or worse, pay no attention to them, we are no longer with them and we have moved from our role as helpers.

With music, as art, there is no reason to believe it can be too good; that would allow us to be satisfied with something less than we are able to do. It gives us more to be aware of: keep in touch with the people who are singing with you. Our choice of keys, arrangements, harmonies, speed, amount to be learned, and type of music all build in things which will either lean us toward performing or leading.

Arrangements which are complicated, or which have the group of leaders singing several parts, can be a distraction for the congregation, especially if they are introduced before the people have a grasp of their part of the song. When the people are best able to sing with you, they will be less conscious of your being "on stage" and will feel more with you and the group. Then they will be able to leave knowing that you were a great help to their expressing their faith, and they will also know that they really did have a chance to pray. If we can accomplish this, we will know we are then a part of that worshipping community: we will be praying with the congregation and the overall parish will be strengthened; we will have "performed" a good service for the Chruch.

With Lyre, Harp
and a Flatpick:

The
Folk
Musician
at
Worship

B. HOW BIG
SHOULD THE MUSIC GROUP BE ?

Six hundred to the left of me,
Six hundred to the right of me,
into the opening song strummed the six hundred . . .

All I can hope is that they were all in tune!

Arranging for an appropriate number of musicians and singers
to lead the congregation is one of the most difficult tasks we perform. Frequently, the group lacks sufficient numbers for members
to support one another — so no one plays. The other side of that
coin, however, is the question of whether we should have nine
guitarists or twelve, to be accompanied by a possible twenty-three
cantors!

The principle should be simple, one of not overdoing a good
thing; but the reality is often that someone might be left out who
is very willing to contribute to the parish liturgy. So let's think
about it a bit. The things involved in your particular situation
and a few ideas should make it possible to come to a good decision
for your own group. We must consider the size of the church. Is
the area you play from large, are you in the sanctuary? When we
take up all the room available, there is a chance that the people
will not be able to see the priest, or at least they will begin to
think his role is somewhat secondary.

Will we be heard? Will the extra people be able to be heard
and therefore add something to the music? Perhaps the most important question to ask is, How many is a song-leader? Is the problem
to provide a leader, or a choir, or an incredible string band?

There are built-in difficulties in making this decision because
of the nature of leading songs and the nature of guitars. The instrument is difficult to tune accurately, and each time another instrument is added the problem is complicated geometrically. Guitar
music is a light sound, even when played with exuberance, and it
is one of precision and clarity because of the plucked nature of the
sound. With these things in mind we notice that when we have
many instruments — six or eight or more guitars played together —

69

With Lyre, Harp
and a Flatpick:
The
Folk
Musician
at
Worship

we are aware of a loss. This loss is often described by some people as something sounding like **mush** — sounds so blended together that nothing is distinguished, neither leader, nor rhythm, nor variation of guitar parts.

"Sorry. Our musicians fill all the pews. You might catch the 10:15 at St. Henry's."

I have heard a few groups which have overcome this mushiness of sound, but I must say the emphasis is on **few**. These groups have done so with great restraint and rehearsal and attention to each other as they play. When they do play, there is a moving toward the fullness of an orchestra rather than the sound of a marching band. While this full orchestral sound is good, we must keep in mind that we are leading music for the people of the congregation, so how many leaders will you **need**?

If I were to think of an ideal, I would suggest the leadership group be composed of one person who can play very well and sing, accompanied by another person playing bass. This arrangement allows for great simplicity because of the space and sound equipment involved. Precision can be worked on to a high degree; movement and other distractions can be kept to a minimum. This is How big? seldom the best arrangement for a parish, so it is likely that the ideal would then be two guitars and a good voice (thus a group of either two or three people). This arrangement allows the singer to concentrate on the people sitting in the pews and the guitarists to give much effort and attention to their playing.

When I think back over the years, it strikes me that one of the best things to happen to me musically was the availability of many good cantors. We were able to use folk music regularly and several different people were interested in singing. I was something of a novice guitar player and generally was terrified when I had to play and sing at the same time — it seemed that one or the other of those responsibilities got short-changed when I had to think about them both at the same time. With the help of different cantors, I was able to get in considerable learning time while we were leading music. There was time to think about the extra licks or really concentrate on the rhythm, or bass notes.

The most rewarding part of it all was the opportunity to gain confidence about playing in front of people — there is now even enjoyment in it for me. The old fear sneaks in occasionally, but it doesn't get out of hand. You may find this dividing of responsibility a good thing for your group to try. Whatever you arrive at, please consider that it is not always a case of the more the merrier or that there is always strength in numbers — especially numbers over four or five.

Surely, this will cause some tensions for you who are leaders or group advisers — tensions from making decisions about who can play best, who should play when, what to do with (or for) those who are interested in helping but lack sufficient experience. The most disastrous thing I could foresee would be to tell someone, "We can't use you now, come back when you get good!" Our groups must have a direction to them, an ability to sustain themselves and go on for a few years. So we must plan how we can develop the talents of those who are interested and at the same time provide the best possible assistance for the congregation of the parish.

With Lyre, Harp
and a Flatpick:
The
Folk
Musician
at
Worship

There are several ways this might be done. The most apparent way to utilize the talents of many musicians is to alternate. If you have two masses when folk music is used, let one group be responsible for one celebration and one for the other; or if there is only one celebration, have the groups alternate Sundays. There is a great advantage to this for the members of the group. It allows them some room for variation of their schedules: it is difficult to be sure everyone can be available for every Sunday of the year and if we can keep the regular responsibility from becoming a burden, the musicians will be able to maintain a freshness, thereby avoiding boredom and the feeling that "we have to play again." I have not often found this attitude in liturgical musicians, but it is something to be aware of and to avoid if possible. As we say over and over, we have taken on a big task in leading music at worship, and people expect a lot, so there is a need for allowing safety valves in the process.

Parish life has a transience about it which is very real: people move, go away to school, join other groups, get jobs at conflicting times. We are, therefore, faced with the unfortunate possibility that our folk group may be here today and gone tomorrow — typically part of the mobile nature of the folk tradition — with the parish left without a very important part of its service to those who come hoping for good music.

Using hypothetical figures and imagined situations, let's try to plan for a group which will be good and also carry itself on. A workable principle for me has always been to use the best musicians available, but to give **all** the musicians experience. By using the best, we provide the greatest assistance for the congregation; along with this core we may include one person of lesser experience or skill who then gets first-hand chance to improve, to learn, and gain familiarity with being in front of a large assembly.

You could set up a system of rotation which would give every musician experience when he is ready. The group would meet regularly and practice together, establishing a challenge to their performing. Additionally, people would be encouraged to work on their music knowing that judgments were being made (although we do not wish to threaten those who are just beginning).

How big?

A good practice is to occasionally invite members of the congregation or outside musicians to listen to the group and evaluate its members individually, especially to indicate the musician who leads well or who best holds the group together. The newer members of the group could be playing regularly at rehearsal meetings and learning from those of longer experience; and they could join the group as their skills increase. I remember in amazement how people who began to play with reluctance became able to take great responsibility within the group and eventually to go on to be leaders of groups.

In the end, it seems we arrive at saying that we want the group to be able to play as a unit and yet with diversified roles. Once we have these roles sufficiently filled, too many extra participants can be a distraction to the congregation: your decisions about your group must be made accordingly.

With Lyre, Harp
and a Flatpick:
The
Folk
Musician
at
Worship

C. DO THE MUSICIANS
PRAY TOO ?

Following from our discussions on "performing," there arises
the question of the musician's personal involvement in worship. It
sometimes seems as though there are so many things to remember
while leading music that it is impossible for the musicians to be at
all involved in actually celebrating. Immediately we should understand that this is an occupational hazard. There is no way for me
to suggest a way of judging anyone's involvement but it seems
necessary for us to remind ourselves occasionally that we have the
opportunity for worship even when we seem to be very busy with
the technical aspects of music. I would hope you are able to pre-
pare enough before services begin that the majority of your concerns
are taken care of. Naturally, we have the responsibility of knowing
what is to come and of thinking ahead. But if we continue to
learn and to reflect on worshipping, our special involvement can
give us the opportunity for greater participation rather than less.
You would very likely find it worthwhile to spend time with the
members of your group thinking over how well you actually participate in liturgy when you are playing.

Some questions which might help clarify your situation would
include: Are we conscious of places where we are asked to respond
in other ways than musically? Are we giving the same attention to
prayers and readings as we continually request of the congregation?
Do we attempt to be aware of the liturgical significance of the songs
we use and the places we sing? And finally — Are we able to occasionally be part of the congregation without being distracted by
not playing?

For the most part, if we are personally involved in the liturgy,
we will add one more dimension to our leadership: that of example.
For very likely, if we are distracted, there is good chance we will
also be distracting the congregation and therefore not helping them.

This area is often the measure by which a great many people evaluate folk music and liturgy. It is another aspect of the responsibility we have accepted as musicians. The more you are able to clearly understand your own participation in worship, the more clearly and helpfully you will be able to discuss questions people have concerning folk music in liturgy.

Do the musicians pray too?

With Lyre, Harp
and a Flatpick:
The
Folk
Musician
at
Worship

D. PLACEMENT OF MUSIC GROUP

Many relationships must be continued over long distances because of work, school, or other unavoidable separations. Although people continue to communicate by phone, letter, and the like, their relationship often progresses more slowly than if the persons involved were near one another. This is particularly true of the relationships of directors of orchestras, plays, choirs, and, you guessed it, those of us who lead congregations in singing. Can you fathom Leonard Bernstein conducting by postcard, or even from the basement of the music hall by yelling through a heating duct?

There have been times when some of our friends have had to do almost that much to be permitted to play in Church. Gradually, we have come to admit that the priest is not the only person active on the altar — lectors, deacons, lay ministers of Communion, and now ourselves as leaders of song have renewed positions in the Church's liturgy. We know that the average congregation can be helped a great deal by having someone lead them in singing, to give them the confidence, encouragement, and invitation to raise their voices in song.

After trying many different arrangements, we have found it helpful, indeed often essential, for the leader of song to be clearly seen and heard if he is to be an effective aid to the congregation. It is nearly impossible to know when to start if the leader is so far away that the people cannot see him or the time lag between his singing and the congregation's hearing causes the whole church to be on different rhythms. He must be readily available, but then be able to disappear gently until the next time he sings. The leader and his group should be in a comfortable, obvious place, one which will add to the balance of the visual effect of the people on the altar, and at the same time allow the celebrant's position to be very clearly demonstrated.

Movement, as the group begins and then leaves, should be minimal, for the purpose of smooth beginnings which eliminate dead space. (This is very important for leading the responses such as acclamations within the Eucharistic prayer.) This movement is an important aspect of placement, and although it may seem strange to us, we should know where each foot is all the time. Our steps should be deliberate enough that the congregation knows we are doing something; movement should be begun when we are about to sing, not during the valuable silent times, and not during the prayers nor the reading of the Scriptures. When it is time, we should execute the move quickly and simply. There may be occasions when we can stay in a place or anticipate a move, particularly for the Eucharistic prayer. It is often possible to move with the introductory greetings to the Preface. People will be invited to stand (or sometimes to move around the altar) and our movement then prepares us to sing the Holy, Holy, and later the Eucharistic acclamation, both of which should begin with the acclamatory burst of song.

Our role comes back to us again: we are responsible and at the same time privileged to lead the congregation; therefore, we must pay close attention to where we are and how we move when we are in front of the group. When it is difficult to get permission to play in front, extra musical effort must be put out so the group will be seen as subtly present when it does get to move in front — the position where they can best be of assistance to the people.

77

With Lyre, Harp
and a Flatpick:
The
Folk
Musician
at
Worship

E. MIKES AND THE LIKE

At the end of a workshop, I had the chance to introduce one of my own songs. I was enjoying it, even remembered all the words. Coming into the last verse, the bassist reached over in front of me and hit the switch — there it was, **sound**, and I had not known that we had been proceeding without it throughout our entire presentation. If this would have happened in a very large church, the parish might not have heard a thing for the entire celebration and as a result been very frustrated. Luckily, in a workshop, things can be repeated if necessary, but this is seldom the case on Sunday in our parishes.

Sound systems generally are categorized in one of two ways: a pleasant addition and great help, or the worst headache going. The really great ones are no trouble to discover: the engineers have managed to do everything but have the microphone follow us around (and even this is available to some); the lesser versions take a lot of attention. But neither system is worth installing if you do not know how to work it.

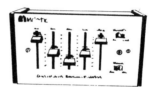

A Microphone Mixer

For the most part, microphones can best be explained by way of illustration, so we have included pictures which should help. The foremost rule for using microphones is: **test them well in advance.** You will then be able to know how close you need to be, and you will find out how much assistance the sound system offers you. An average microphone works well for as many as three people if they stand close together. Our best teachers on getting maximum usage from a single microphone are the members of Blue Grass bands. If you have ever had the opportunity to see good Blue Grass music performed live, you will have noticed that always three and sometimes four or five musicians will be huddled around a single microphone. This is not optimum for liturgists but, when necessary, we can make do in a similar fashion.

79

With Lyre, Harp
and a Flatpick:
The
Folk
Musician
at
Worship

A microphone system can be a help and a friend. Obtain the right kind, and it will be neither a distraction nor a nightmare.

You will find that some microphones work only if you are within one or two inches of them. Others pick up well from six to eight inches (and would probably distort if you spoke too closely to them). I encourage you to keep trying to get the most from your church's sound system. If, however, after many attempts the system is still unsatisfactory, you might suggest that additional microphones or stronger power amplifiers be purchased. Sometimes several microphones can be used together by purchasing inexpensive mixers (c.f., illustration). Many churches cannot afford the kind of equipment that would be most helpful to folk musicians, but if good music is indeed a priority in your church, some provision must be made to improve the sound system. Do whatever you must to obtain sufficient equipment so that the congregation may hear you. I hope you will use all of your ingenuity in this regard. Plot if you must but make sure people can hear you.

F.
COOPERATING
WITH
THE
CELEBRANT

The initial effort required to bring smoothness to celebrations might give us the feeling of being technicians or stage hands in a drama. But we get less conscious of our functional responsibilities to the extent that we are able to integrate our attentiveness to how we perform as leaders with our attentiveness to ourselves and our neighbor, the congregation. As this integration becomes more complete, the actions of singing, listening and movement will become more fully symbols of our faith and the presence of Christ in our community.

The smooth coordination of our actions results in those acts becoming a unified symbol. Underlying this symbolism is coordinated planning among all those responsible for leading the liturgy — priest, lector, servers and musicians. We are able to move smoothly when we know what each other is doing.

Is she going to read a psalm?

Will we sing the Our Father?

Will he be disturbed if we sing all the verses?

How many more verses are they going to sing?

Are they going to sing the responses?

Common uncertainties such as the above CAN be eliminated by means of a few moments spent together before the celebration or with a written guide. (A combination of both methods is most effective.) Freed from functional doubts and anxieties, we can be more at ease with one another during the liturgy. The leaders of the celebration can cover one another and move *with* each other.

The importance of smooth planning and communication is heightened by the simple fact that there still can be changes in the original plan called for by sheer circumstance. If we know what we are doing, we can allow these things to be taken in stride without a total disruption of the flow of the celebration.

A good example is the need for flexibility in the song(s) planned during the distribution of Communion. Since we never really know how long it will take, we should be prepared to add or take away verses or even a whole song.

If proper planning has been done, there will not be the sudden trauma of the priest turning toward you as he says the last syllable of the introduction to the Eucharistic Acclamation, and expecting you to sing. (Even in such emergencies, it certainly adds to the celebration if you can keep your wits together and begin a version of the acclamation!) On the other hand, our planning should not be so rigid that we would panic if the mood and flow of the celebration called for the priest or other leader to offer spontaneous commentary or a prayer at a time when we had planned to begin a song. And — whoever *planned* to break a guitar string?

83

5

Things to do more than five minutes before a Liturgy

A. PLANNING . . . PLANNING . . . PLANNING . . .

Folk musicians have a long tradition of living very existentially and capturing whatever is available in a moment's need. I'm sure it is not always by choice. For some reason or other, even when we think we have planned, many things happen which cause us to plan all over again on the spot. It strikes me that there will never be any old liturgical musicians if we do not learn how to plan right: we will all die of last-minute tensions!

A few weeks ago I was invited to play for a grade school graduation. Since the group was very organized, they called me three days before the event was to take place, suggesting six songs, three of which I had played before and three of which I had never heard. I agreed to play on the condition that they mail me the music. We also agreed that we would practice with the grade school students on the morning of the day of graduation. Time rolled on and soon it was Wednesday and time to play. Still no music in the mail. Figuring that somehow or other the Lord would provide, I packed up my guitar and copies of the songs

With Lyre, Harp
and a Flatpick:
The
Folk
Musician
at
Worship

that I knew, and left for the school. Because they were so efficient and I was behind schedule, they started rehearsal without me. They ended up teaching me the songs and somehow or other, by the evening, the celebration occurred almost without a hitch. Except one slight slip.

During our rehearsal with the parents, we practiced the scripture response and one other song, then began to practice the opening song (with Communion and ending songs still to be learned). There we were, learning the opening song, when suddenly a huge procession began marching down the aisle. At that point rehearsal was ended and the liturgy had begun!

If the tensions which come from such occurrences are to be avoided, we must, at least, develop a reliable planning procedure which allows us to be prepared for most eventualities. Such a procedure considers the following preparations:

Planning . . .
planning . . .
planning . . .

* **What songs
will we sing?**

* **How much time
will we have to learn and practice them?**

* **How early
will we be given the music?**

* **Who will be playing with us?**

* **Will there be time for rehearsal?**

* **Who will be
in the congregation?**

* **Will the congregation
be familiar with the songs?**

* **What music
will be in the hands of the congregation?**

* **Which of us
will play which part of which song?**

If these questions are given reasonable time for consideration, the overall result will be a much smoother and expressive celebration of liturgy. It is easy to systematize our planning and if we give it adequate time, we can avoid such traumatic occurrences as our graduation scene. It does not seem reasonable to push our luck, hoping that things will "work out just right." We can count on making a small number of last-minute decisions, but these should concern only those things we **plan** to do and are unable to carry out.

**With Lyre, Harp
and a Flatpick:**
The
Folk
Musician
at
Worship

Planning must be done in a way that fits your own style, but I have found the following considerations consistently helpful:

1. **Take advantage of as much time as is given to you.**
   Because many of us do play weekly, there is not a great deal of time between masses for planning. You may find that planning several weeks in advance (or perhaps a month's celebrations) will be helpful.
   If this is impossible, it is good to at least begin planning at the end of any Sunday. If either of these methods is used, you will have a head start on your rehearsal meetings.

2. Keep records of when songs are used.

Because we all have our favorites, it is very easy to find yourself singing the same five or six songs many times in the course of a month. If we have some sort of record (planning sheet or chart), we will know when we are singing a song too often.

3. Prepare an outline.

Any number of forms are available which simplify the listing of everything that will be done in a given service. Many people design their own outlines; others simply write down what they've decided to do for that week. In either case such an outline is an extremely useful tool in coordinating the efforts of musicians, readers, and the celebrant. It removes doubt about who is taking care of what and permits a smooth flow between recited and sung parts of the liturgy.

Planning . . .
planning . . .
planning . . .

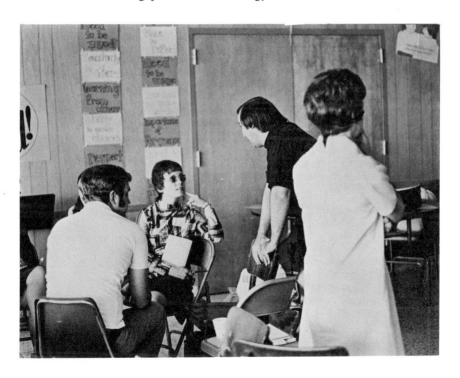

With Lyre, Harp
and a Flatpick:
The
Folk
Musician
at
Worship

With these principles in mind, we can see that planning gives us the added advantage of being more personally confident as we lead the singing. I'm sure that many of you welcome any assistance with the continual occupational hazard of stage fright. When we know **before** the service exactly what we will teach, what songs the people know well, when we will be moving — we increase our self-assurance, as well as the congregation's confidence in us as leaders.

Example of a Planning Sheet for liturgies

B. EVALUATION
AND CRITICISM

Chapter Five:
Things
to do
more
than
five minutes
before
a liturgy

If I were ever to purchase a soap-box for the purpose of speaking loud and long, it would be used to advocate evaluation and criticism. Since I now have the opportunity, I will take advantage of my "soap-box" for a few lines. I began this discussion in the section on *Various Responses* earlier, but hardly feel it was sufficient to cover such an important area thoroughly. Criticism and evaluation are not only among the most helpful tools we have; they are **essential** if we hope to defeat mediocrity. With help and concentration on criticism, we will automatically continue to become better as we play.

Criticism is really quite simple, consisting of a single rule: Listen very carefully to everything you play, and be willing to change in the interest of improvement.

Since we have just completed thinking about planning, we can presume that you **chose** to do certain things. Therefore, the evaluation becomes simple: did you do what you wanted to do? As far as arrangements go, it is simple to determine when we have done the song as arranged. Usually, the only problem is remembering to take the time to do the evaluating. This can easily be accomplished when we are rehearsing for the next liturgy. The only question remaining is: Are we really interested in doing better? If we continually do not examine what we are doing, there is reason to believe we are only half interested in progress. You alone can be the judge in this case. I hope you will find your own system of evaluation rather than making it necessary for others to come to you when things get really bad.

91

With Lyre, Harp
and a Flatpick:
The
Folk
Musician
at
Worship

If you have not thought about HOW to criticize your playing or presentation of songs, allow me to suggest some key points which will be helpful. The most important areas to consider are:

- ☐ playing right

- ☐ singing right

- ☐ consistency

- ☐ pace

- ☐ key

- ☐ clarity — notes and words

- ☐ arrangement

- ☐ feeling — mood, tone

- ☐ expression of faith

- ☐ concern for the congregation

- ☐ volume — dynamics of loud and soft

- ☐ rhythm

- ☐ unity

- ☐ beginnings, endings, refrains

- ☐ length of songs

Without spending pages and pages commenting on each of these, let us try to arrive at some principles which will be useful to you in these areas of criticism.

Celebrations which we plan can be easily judged if we arrive at a system of obtaining information about our part in the service. One of the most effective ways of obtaining such information is by using a tape recorder, either video or audio. You can tape either rehearsals or actual celebrations. They can then be replayed and analyzed to see what went well and what went badly.

A machine like the one on the Left can give you *some* idea of how you are doing. One like the model pictured on the Right won't lie to you and is fairly easy to borrow. The parish should own one anyway.

We need to say here that the mention of <u>well</u> is as important as the mention of <u>badly</u>, for if we are not aware of our strengths, we will have nothing to build on. By acknowledging the things we do well, we gain the ambition and confidence to continue trying new things. So don't wear yourselves out with negatives and forget that you are already offering something to the congregation, that the criticism is aimed at making services better.

One way to stimulate discussion of good and bad points is to have occasional help from outsiders, as we mentioned briefly in an earlier section. We have lately added a special session to workshops when the local musicians play for each other in simulated services. One group of participants is the "congregation" and the individual groups of musicians become leaders of that "parish." After the leaders play or teach a song, doing several verses, the audience is invited to comment on all parts of the performance. Comments range from discussion of the value of the song, to the clarity of pronunciation, to all the others we have listed above. People even mention whether the group seems to like the song or if they are very much "into it."

93

With Lyre, Harp
and a Flatpick:

The
Folk
Musician
at
Worship

You could perform a tremendous service to the parish folk musicians in your area if you were to plan to meet with them once a month or so, trade songs, and comment on each other's music and presentation. We are attempting such a project in the Cincinnati Archdiocese and will let you know how it progresses. You might find that this would be like having lessons — and in a sense it is, because you are providing yourself with time for learning.

By this type of evaluation and work, you will learn to become critical and careful about what you are doing. You should then be able to increase your attention to music and the many aspects involved in effective leadership as a musician.

Rev. Carey Landry, prolific composer and a leading speaker and educator on the matter of good taste, critical appraisal and pastoral/liturgical worth in contemporary music for worship.

C. THE SONGS THEMSELVES —
CHOOSING AND EVALUATING
(Themes and other Considerations)

Chapter Five:
Things
to do
more
than
five minutes
before
a liturgy

Over the years various systems have been developed for choosing music. As we look back, it was usually a special occasion when we were able to use folk music in our worship services. These occasions were often connected with such things as graduations, youth groups, and other organizations, openings and closings of the school year or retreats. In these situations we very naturally wished to choose songs appropriate to the occasion. As the use of folk music has become more widespread, the method of choosing songs has remained — organizing around a theme.

This is a method which is used by many people planning all types of liturgical celebrations. It is very useful and likely gives us the best help for arranging unified and integrated services. I am sure you are familiar with the approaches to thematic planning. The first is to check the readings assigned to the day. Beginning here we have a core to build on. Considering the readings and important events of the parish, we can arrive at a clear expression of some aspect of our faith.

95

With Lyre, Harp
and a Flatpick:

The
Folk
Musician
at
Worship

The other method which has developed out of special situations is one of choosing a theme based on the cause of celebration, the group gathered, or other sacraments. In these situations we will take our theme and search the scripture for readings which are closely related or clearly express the idea we have chosen. The planning of music follows very similarly in this method.

Both of these methods prove to be very helpful and we should always use one or the other. The one possible caution that might be stated is when we celebrate in the context of Eucharist, we already have a unifying thread woven within it. That thread is the basic and constant idea of praise and thanksgiving which is the very meaning of Eucharist. Because we as Catholic Christians are so familiar with Eucharist as our "normal" form of worship, there is sometimes a tendency to wrap a great variety of ideas and themes around Eucharist to the total disguise of this part of our worship. If we are able to keep this in mind, our planning will result in a greater depth of expression.

When we limit ourselves to vague theme topics such as joy, celebration, or friendship, our worship tends to become worn out. These are very important themes of our Christianity and they deserve attention; but the idea deserves to be something more than superficial. But, because these themes are so important, we must remember that they contain many subordinate aspects, and to attempt to cover all of them at once is more than we can expect. If we are able to look at important aspects of any of these large topics, we will avoid the vagueness which can occur when we attempt to cover too much too quickly.

For example, I am often asked to play for weddings. When the time comes for a planning session, I will often ask the couple if they have a particular message they would like to express by way of the liturgy. The question itself often comes as a surprise because many people are still not used to planning celebrations. (We have an excellent opportunity to give them a chance to learn as we are planning.) After thinking about the question briefly, often they might say something like "our love for each other." Discussion will often help them say more clearly what "our love for each other" means for them, for example "our commitment of trust or support." Arriving at this more specified theme, we can then proceed to choose songs and readings which are best suited for their wedding celebration. It is possible then to emphasize both the sacrament which they celebrate as a couple as well as the sacrament of Eucharist which we celebrate as a community.

If we plan with these things in mind, we avoid what some would consider being forced to plan around a structure. When the structure becomes burdensome, we would do well to consider other liturgical forms. We have options for celebrating special occasions such as weddings and baptisms. They can take place within the celebration of Eucharist but can also be celebrated very well on their own. If you are helping people plan, it is well to remind them of these options. Surely, we will be ahead if the forms we are using help us to communicate our meaning rather than cause an inconsistency by imposing more messages than a single form is able to contain.

Within our special plannings, there is often an additional requirement for our being very critical of the songs we use. When people come to us to ask us to play, they come with great divergence of musical knowledge and taste. Some are very well versed in the songs which are most frequently used for liturgy. Others are not at all familiar with contemporary music. Whichever is the case, we must help them make good decisions on what is appropriate.

Hundreds of folk-style songs with a liturgical motif have been published in recent years, and there are many more which come to us from the popular music field, and still more which have been composed by friends and, often, ourselves. As these resources become ever more plentiful, it becomes ever more important for us to be able to make some kind of evaluative judgement of a song's worth. We know there are songs in this idiom which have become classics, and we know too that there are some which have been quite popular but which grate against our sensitivities.

We do have to be able to make some fundamental evaluation of the music we use. There are basic criteria to help us, but no easy-reference charts, ratings, or other simple methods. It is good

With Lyre, Harp
and a Flatpick:
The
Folk
Musician
at
Worship

to notice suggestions for songs which frequently appear in articles, newsletters and other resources offered as aids in planning celebrations. The Bishops' Statement, *Music in Catholic Worship* (see Ch. 9, page 131 in this book), offers three major areas for evaluation of music: Musical, Liturgical, Pastoral.

The guidelines which the bishops have outlined for liturgical music very likely give us the best starting place. For music to be effective for worship, it must be good music, it must fit liturgically, and it must be pastorally helpful to those who are using it. These guidelines will help us choose music which is consistent with our ideals as musicians and liturgists. We must decide intelligently whether a song contains musical quality. Some of that judgment is based on taste but much of it is based on long-standing principles. For example, the melody and the words must be integrated and learnable. Songs can be judged liturgically useful if they genuinely aid our expression of our Christianity and are consistent with the action they accompany.

My long-time favorite example of a mistake in liturgical planning happened again last week. A group asked me to play "Sounds of Silence" for a communion hymn. While Paul Simon wrote an excellent song, one clearly pointing out some of the difficulties we experience in an alienated society, it hardly seems appropriate to "celebrate" that alienation as we are expressing our unity in the most complete way we have — the sharing of the Body and Blood of the Lord. That song, however, may have appropriate use in another context.

As for determining whether a song is pastorally appropriate, we must consider who will be invited to sing it, what the occasion is, and how much the majority of the people will benefit by its use. There are times when we might even have to admit that the very use of folk music would be pastorally inappropriate, although I believe that a good introduction and helpful song leading would negate that principle. Individual songs, nevertheless, deserve attention when we are choosing. If a song has too many associations to other events, very likely it would not be wise to choose it. For example, "Silent Night" is so associated with Christmas that we would not sing it on Easter. The clash of associations would prove distracting.

If you will keep in mind that people are usually less than familiar with the procedure of planning celebrations, and that your experience can help them learn a great deal, and if you remain aware of the principles for criticizing music and the relatedness of themes and Eucharist, you will, I am sure, be able to be of great assistance to them when they plan. You will also be better able to offer well-planned liturgies for the Sunday services you might be involved with on a regular basis. If you keep evaluating and keep searching, your music program will develop and avoid stagnation.

MUSICAL JUDGEMENT brings up many different questions about a song. Do you like it? Do you think you could learn it? Can a congregation learn it? Is the voice range reasonable? Are the words speakable? Do they make sense? Do they have an element of the poetic? Will they wear out with one use? Would you sing the song personally? Is the melody appealing? Does the melody bring out the meaning and mood of the words? Does the arrangement of the song lend itself well to available instrumentation and voices? And so forth. The longer you play, the more instinctive this basic musical judgement will become. When in doubt, get help from other musicians.

The LITURGICAL JUDGEMENT requires additional questions, the primary one being whether the song has a real connection to what we celebrate in our worship. This question must be answered rather specifically and it applies to songs both "liturgical" and "commercial" — neither category is excused from this criticism. No one

With Lyre, Harp
and a Flatpick:
The
Folk
Musician
at
Worship

generally expects you to give a theological treatise or biblical egegesis on a song, but you should be able to relate it to what you believe when you celebrate. Other questions might be: does it fit in this particular celebration? Does it belong in some specific place within the celebration (i.e. Communion, Scripture Response, etc.)? Does the song help overall as we try to enable people to respond in faith and to grow in that faith?

The PASTORAL JUDGEMENT is for the benefit of everyone. Is the song going to be helpful for this congregation at this time? This requires insight into the overall situation. Here is where it is most important that we have met the congregation and know things which are helpful. Points which you might remember would be: can they learn it today; will this song overload the rehearsal time or unbalance the celebration? Will the song be understandable? Here the tone of the words must be looked at again. If a song is very strong, it may need more introduction than most; it may require longer time to be understood before it is introduced. Most songs which are good music and fit well liturgically will be able to be used with almost any congregation — BUT you will not be able to introduce every song at the same time or as quickly as others. Stay close to them, and you will know best.

6

When We Actually Begin

A. GENTLE CHALLENGE —
DON'T WAIT TOO LONG!

When we are teaching music and working with the parish, we are eager to have people learn a number of new songs and to sing them well; but in our eagerness we risk expecting too much from people and thus leaving them behind. We should push them a little but be ready to wait for them as they come along. In this way, we will expand their knowledge of songs and their strength as singers; and, most of all, we will prevent boredom from setting in.

This boredom is potentially the most damaging thing that can happen to celebrations. When people are no longer interested in what they are singing, they sing with very little enthusiasm and are unwilling to learn new songs. But if we develop as musicians and leaders of song, our skill and presentation will be increasingly inviting to the congregation, and they will be less likely to be bored.

As people are invited to sing, they may well be surprised at how much they can learn. Most people have a low estimation of how well they can sing. We want to be very careful not to permit

With Lyre, Harp
and a Flatpick:
The
Folk
Musician
at
Worship

them to continue thinking that they are poor singers who cannot improve. If we are teaching properly, if the music is well organized, if the people are aware of our concern for their learning, they will be able to learn far more than they ever expected. Why not give them a chance to be astounded at themselves!

The principle we are working with here is that we once learned it; we have no reason to expect that the people can't. With this principle in mind, think a moment of the pace with which your musical learning has taken place. You probably learned when the music seemed new or exciting or very worthwhile — perhaps you heard a particular song or version which caught your attention. When this happened, you may have gone home and spent several hours working through the new arrangement or learning whatever new patterns were necessary to do the song. We must assume that the congregation will be invited to learn more about music in the same fashion we did. If our music is exciting, the congregation will be encouraged to join us, but we must also remember that we work hard to perfect our arrangements and we should allow the congregation similar time.

Occasionally, you might offer a special musical arrangement to the congregation. They will probably enjoy a chance to do a round or to add harmony to a song they are already familiar with. These arrangements can be very useful for acclamations like the Great Amen or responses during the liturgy of the word. Special arrangements need to be introduced carefully and people must have a chance to learn them thoroughly or they may become very disappointed with the results. With it all, remember to add a note of urgency to their learning. It will remind them that we don't have forever to make songs good.

B. "SING IT LIKE YOU BELIEVE IT!"

Nothing we do is more indicative of our willingness to be part of the worshipping community than the way we present ourselves and our beliefs as we sing. When we are really involved in a song, people will know it, and they will know when we are genuinely interested. Therefore, we should believe what we are singing.

Sometimes our abilities to lead the music with enthusiasm are severely taxed. For example, within a two or three week period we may be invited to play for weekly service and a wedding and a graduation. Invariably, we are asked to play several of the same songs. Even when the songs are good ones — not only popular but worthwhile musically and liturgically — they become worn out from overuse. When this happens, we are faced with a problem — how to sing the song as it was intended so that it will be helpful to the parish.

When songs are selected for a celebration, we should be willing to remind people that some songs have experienced greater wear than others; and, I believe, we should even be willing to tell them that some songs are worn out either for us personally or for the congregation. It is difficult, however, to disregard the wishes of people who are planning special celebrations. We need to inform them so they may make good judgments but there will be times when it is important to use a song they choose. When this happens, we are challenged. We have to refresh whatever good experience we have had with a song. Since it an important song for the people who have chosen it, we must try to lead it as well as we know how.

Remember, we cannot expect the congregation to respond with more enthusiasm than we show as leaders. We will surely determine how well a congregation will sing by how well we lead it. If it is obvious that we are even slightly bored with a song,

103

With Lyre, Harp
and a Flatpick:
The
Folk
Musician
at
Worship

the congregation will sense our boredom. If, however, they see our enthusiasm, they will know that the song was chosen because of its value and that we are offering it to them in their interest as well as the interest of the special celebration.

It might be worthwhile to return once again to our chapter on music and symbol to refresh and possibly further our thoughts on why we play. As we continue to see ourselves as genuinely interested in assisting the people of the parish, we will show our conviction as we sing. A severe guideline might be: "If you don't believe it, don't sing it." This can cause difficulties for people who are planning but, at the same time, we should presume that we believe those things we sing. Without that presumption, we lose both honesty and consistency.

C. ENNUNCIATION

Several years ago many of us had the opportunity to see the story of Eliza Doolittle as she learned to speak English properly and become "My Fair Lady." Professor Higgins offered many exercises to help her speak correctly. My favorite scene is the one in which Eliza has a mouthful of marbles and at the same time is forced to speak very clearly. At one point, she swallows one of the marbles and moans to Professor Higgins. In patient understanding, he very seriously tells her: "That's quite all right; I have plenty more."

I don't recommend that you choke on marbles or endure any other such torture to help you speak but, in your own creativeness, be sure that you devise some way to concentrate on clarity so the congregation can hear every syllable you speak. As strange as it seems, extra work devoted to clear enunciation will pay off. Even though we are sure that we look like we're overdoing it, people will respond only pleasantly when they notice that they can hear what is being sung.

With Lyre, Harp
and a Flatpick:
The
Folk
Musician
at
Worship

Here is an enunciation exercise that might be helpful to you. Try standing in front of a mirror as you sing a song, read, or recite. First, try it very casually and then try it with utmost concentration on the sounds. It may look strange and feel worse, but you will find that the more you concentrate on clear diction the less strained it will be.

I believe it is possible to speak clearly and to sing in such a way that people can understand what you say even without straining every muscle in your face. No doubt it will help if you stretch these muscles, but the point is you need to **think** about the sounds you are saying so they are clearly sung or spoken.

Speaking clearly — getting the sound of your voice outside yourself — is called "projection" by speech and drama teachers. Projection has ramifications for us as leaders of liturgical music. Besides the simple emission of sounds from our vocal chords, we also communicate the symbol and energy of which we spoke earlier when we "project."

When we are working in a group, we can help other members of the group with enunciation and projection. When we notice that one of the members is singing with little or no effort, he usually is not concentrating on what he is singing. And as we have said over and over, if we are not concentrating on our singing, we are not going to be helpful to the people who are relying on us. So, if you feel that your face is strained more than it should be, you're probably not quite straining it enough, which is to say the more you work on your diction and clarity of speech, the better it will be for your congregation.

Because we deal with such mechanical monsters as public address systems, we must give additional consideration to what is done with our voice after we turn it loose. We may be speaking clearly but, if a PA system causes a good deal of reverberation, then we must allow for this and plan accordingly. To find out about PA distortion, check with people before or after celebrations so that they will help you evaluate how clearly sounds carry over the system.

D. EYE CONTACT

If you have ever been instructed in public speaking, you have undoubtedly been told to make good eye contact with your audience. I wholeheartedly believe in eye contact in the liturgical music context, but for reasons other than those given by speech teachers. It **is** important to meet the eyes of your audience in order to establish rapport and to let them know you are interested in communicating to them. But, also, eye contact helps us understand the congregation's response to the music, their involvement in the singing, their possible dissatisfaction, or their keen pleasure.

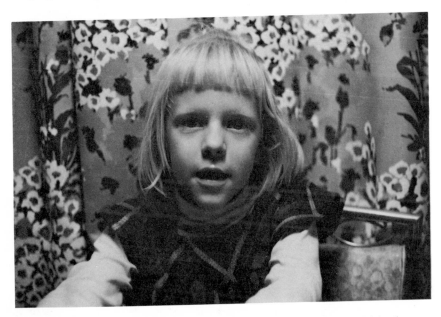

Ideally, we would like to have a running dialogue with the congregation, but the size of churches as well as natural inhibitions prevents us from always conducting such an exchange. We can, however, use our eyes to evaluate the congregation's response to the music. If we see that the group is bored with the song, we must find out why. If they are lost as we teach, we must correct whatever is hindering their learning. If they really like the song, we want to know that as well. Since this kind of response is a treat, why miss it when it occurs?

With Lyre, Harp
and a Flatpick:
The
Folk
Musician
at
Worship

I should add as an addendum to this discussion of eye contact that another important reason for maintaining visual contact is that it encourages the congregation's participation. When they know that we are with them as they sing, they join in more willingly and energetically.

If it is difficult for you to remember to look at the congregation, particularly if doing so increases your stage fright, you might find it helpful to keep notes on the music which will remind you at certain points to look at the people — in spite of your fears. The notes, rests, key signatures and other musical symbols are there to help us; written reminders are no less important if we are to do the important things which make for better music and singing.

7

Technology and Symbol Coming Alive

A. RIGHT TUNE: WRONG KEY

Have you ever imagined what it feels like to be a bass note on a pipe organ? Imagine yourself with vocal chords of 16 feet or 32 feet. To make these notes vibrate, vast quantities of air are required and in the end the note produced is sometimes one which is hardly distinguishable from others.

We often require our congregations to expand their normal singing ranges to as low as those bass notes. It is no surprise, therefore, that the congregation's singing seems to lack spirit. All of their concentration is required in acquiring air for those nebulous low notes. Who would have the energy to add any spirit to a song? So, often by a simple change of key it is possible for us to add a whole new mood to a song and to invigorate the singing of the congregation. Singing in the right range is almost as important as singing the right song. For if people are **unable** to sing with us, we are surely wasting our time trying to lead the song.

With Lyre, Harp
and a Flatpick:
The
Folk
Musician
at
Worship

When we choose a key for a song, we chance erring in two equally, but differently, bad ways. If we set the song in a range that is too **low**, the congregation becomes bored and will pay little attention to what the song can mean for them. If, on the other hand, we set the song in a range that is too **high**, they will be forced to strain their voices and give up in frustration.

Because of the nature of many songs, we often struggle with fine lines of too high or too low. I believe that we are better off to challenge the congregation slightly on the high end rather than put them to sleep on the low end. Stretching our singing range slightly at the top can add excitement to a song, but be very careful that you do not cause the congregation to end up leaving with sore throats.

We are generally safe if we choose keys which allow people to sing in a middle range. This would include middle C and the octave above. Any group of singers can easily be comfortable within that range. If we are lucky enough to be singing with people later in the day, we can sometimes count on one note on each end of that octave. You will have to determine what leeway you have with your group by taking into consideration such things as age, sex, and experience of those with whom you are singing.

Put in terms of a guitar, you will find that the keys of E-flat, F, and G are among the most useful singing keys, but unfortunately E-flat and F are very difficult keys for the guitarist. The guitar is simply not designed to give its best performance in these keys. For this reason we have the invention of the sometimes notorious implement known as the **capo**. If you have never used one, I suggest you immediately purchase one. If you have used one, I hope you have paid some attention to its helpfulness.

The capo permits us to use the good sounding and first learned chords on the guitar. By learning chords for three keys (C, G, and D), you are able to play in any of the standard musical keys, and therefore accomodate the range of almost any congregation.

We need to take a brief look at the technical reason the capo is so helpful. By placing the capo on any fret of the guitar, you are able to raise the pitch of the song. For each fret that the capo is raised, the key will also be raised one-half step. So, if we recall that E-flat is a good singing key for a particular song but we only know chords for the key of C, we know we could count from C to E-flat (C; C♯; D; E-flat) and find that there are three half steps between. By placing the capo on the third fret and playing the appropriate C chords, we will then be playing in the true sounding key of E-flat.

While there is a theoretical explanation as we have described it, you will best understand the way the capo works as you experiment yourself. Very likely, many songs which you learn in the key of C or A-minor will be much more comfortable for yourself and members of the congregation if you raise them two or three frets on the guitar. It is often helpful to try any song in several keys even though the first key may seem reasonable. There is always the possibility that you will discover added spirit by changing the key in which you are singing.

The one hazard which is involved in using a capo is that its use can cause the guitar to become slightly out of tune. This is particularly true of capos which are the most effective, those that hold the strings tightly enough so they will not buzz and yet lightly enough that they are not stretched to a different pitch. When you use the capo or remove it, always be sure to check and see if any notes have changed. As you gain facility with the capo, you will become more able to apply it and notice whether or not the strings are stretched or bent. Placing the capo properly will eliminate the majority of difficulties. As should be standard practice, pay scrupulous attention to the accuracy of tuning. I cannot overemphasize how important good tuning is. If you do nothing else, at least have the guitar in tune.

If you have not been playing for a long time, you may find tuning difficult, but my experience has been that the more familiar you are with the sound of the guitar the more precisely

111

With Lyre, Harp
and a Flatpick:

The
Folk
Musician
at
Worship

you can determine which pitch is correct for each string. It takes patience and sometimes you will wish that it were possible to tune your guitar once and then weld the keys, but until then, we will continue to contend with all the things which cause the guitar to be out of tune — weather, capos, old strings, and people running into one another!

Additional examples of the usefulness of the capo are provided in the Appendix. For example, you can very often produce excellent variations in accompaniment by having two guitars play in different keys and using a capo to bring the sounds into harmony. A song is arranged this way for practice on page 161.

Ideally, we would be accomplished enough to play in keys which do not require capos. Ideally, we would have the full range of "bar chords" at our command. In any case, the capo is a legitimate aid to creative and flexible playing of the guitar.

"Transposing" a song from one key to another is frequently desirable. A guide to understanding how to transpose in also included in the Appendix.

B. THE FOUNDATION OF ACCOMPANIMENT

During my career as a marching musician, I had the outstanding opportunity to play a most refined and delicate instrument: the sousaphone (more commonly called the tuba). Besides learning a great deal about breathing large quantities of air, I came to appreciate the musical value of all those oompahs.

Because the rhythm and accents of a song are so important, we often need an instrument designed solely to emphasize them. In the folk tradition rhythm is provided by the bass. The varieties which are most commonly known to us are bass fiddle or electric bass (and on rare occasions the washtub bass). If you have a choice of any instrument to add to your group, your first one should be a bass. It will add depth to the musical accompaniment and will give great assistance to the congregation in terms of constant rhythm. If you will announce your need for a bass musician or plead with the congregation, you may find an experienced musician who is willing to help you out as bassist. If this does not happen, perhaps one member of the group might be willing to learn bass. Anyone with more than minimum familiarity with the guitar should have no great difficulty learning the bass. Its value to your group will be very clear.

In addition to recognizing the value of bass accompaniment, the folk musician should be able to make the most of the rich bass notes possible within the chord structures of his own playing. See the Appendix for further explanation.

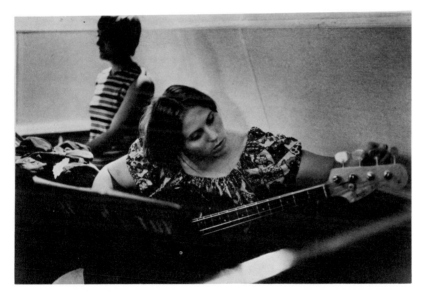

LOU ANDERSON's talent with both acoustical and electric bass guitar has enriched many liturgies, concerts and recording sessions, including popular albums by Joe Wise, Neil Blunt, Jack Miffleton and Fr. Carey Landry.

113

With Lyre, Harp
and a Flatpick:
The
Folk
Musician
at
Worship

C. RHYTHM:
SPEED KILLS!

The pace of a song very likely will determine whether or not it is alive. Singing too slowly will probably bore the congregation; singing too quickly will wear them out. Given the right of individual interpretation of a song, I am reluctant to suggest that any song must have a definite speed, but we must *decide* on the speed and remain consistent with it or people will not know what to expect from the next line.

As you develop musically, you will notice many different speeds and rhythms that are available to choose from. You will do well to learn several of them. The most obvious responsibility is one of knowing differences between 3/4 and 4/4 time. Occasionally, playing in the wrong time is the cause of songs being very difficult to learn. A friend of mine reminds me sadly that his group still plays *Amazing Grace* in 4/4 time. Not only does such an error make it difficult for us to learn songs but it also completely confuses the congregation.

When you use different rhythms, be aware of the places that are accented. Proper accent can make all the difference for the congregation. It is possible by using the wrong accent to thoroughly disguise the mood intended by an author. Therefore, it is a good idea to work on being comfortable with several strums or finger picking styles. This allows you the freedom to give any song somewhat individual treatment. Above all, be critical enough to prevent every song's becoming monotonously similar. I have tried to suggest some alternatives for you to learn. I hope you will find them helpful. By choosing and remembering the speed for any song, we add another bit to our consistency and ability to add strength and confidence to the songs.

D. BEGINNINGS AND ENDINGS OF SONGS

Liturgical celebrations have a way of moving within several levels of spirit, ranging from quiet meditation to enthusiastic response. If the shifts from one level to another are to be made well, we must allot time for transition.

Any time we sing we should be aware of transitions. The beginning of a song provides a shift from either silence or speaking. With the introduction, we attempt to bring the people into the song both musically and personally. We want to make sure we offer sufficient time for them to make the transition.

The introduction is not a time when we decide on our rhythm or on which note we will begin to sing; rather it is a help to move into a song. I am sure you all will recall times when a new song would have a very long introduction, with you and other members of the group looking at each other with great fear and wondering where and when to begin. You will probably find that deciding on the introduction beforehand and rehearsing it that way will eliminate this hesitation and unsureness from beginnings.

With Lyre, Harp
and a Flatpick:
The
Folk
Musician
at
Worship

Once you have begun the song it should proceed properly until the end, the time of another transition. The ending allows the people to get out of the song and into the next section of the service. By paying attention to endings, we eliminate the jarring effect caused by abruptness.

The best way to end a song is to allow for the speed to slow and the last notes to fade on their own. If we are willing to stand for an extra ten seconds or so as we have ended a song, we will provide for ourselves and the congregation to conclude the song and to be ready for the next part.

Be very careful that you do not play the last note and immediately stop the strings on your guitar as you walk away. This leaves the song somewhat unfinished (we are still enjoying the last bits), and can draw undue attention to your presence. If we steal the music from the congregation while they are savoring it, we do a disservice to them. Very simply: leave them a little space.

E. HARMONY

We have spoken previously of the question of musical virtuosity in liturgy — the "how good is too good" problem. Our basic principle is that we should offer music that is as good as we are capable of. One exception to that injunction is in the use of harmony. Although it usually is a great asset, it can hinder complete learning and good singing by the congregation if it is overdone or introduced at the wrong time.

Generally, harmony can be used very freely when the group is singing on its own (for example, during verses or in meditative songs). On the refrains, however, and especially if a song is new, some caution should be practiced when introducing harmony. On some occasions it is very worthwhile to teach different parts to the congregation but be sure that they are able to learn it strongly and will be able to follow someone within the group. Your knowledge of the congregation and good judgment will be the way to decide when the more complex versions of songs can be used.

Possible starting points may be to introduce a simple harmony for the Great Amen, or using songs or refrains which can be sung as a round. People enjoy and gain confidence in singing rounds, but be sure you are in control of when to start!

Respondez-vous s'il vous plâit!

A. CONGREGATIONAL PARTICIPATION:
ANTIPHONS vs. COMPLETE HYMNS

The structure of most folk songs emphasizes simplicity with considerable repetition to aid learning. This style of song with the frequency of antiphon or refrain raises the question of how much the congregation should be expected to sing. I am sure that many of us have spent time discussing or arguing about whether to teach a whole song or simply the refrain. Many feel that they are leaving the congregation out when they are asking them to sing only a refrain.

Personally, I think this question has an evolving answer. In the interest of good learning, teaching small sections of the song over an extended period of time will be the best approach. Very often, members of the congregation will make their own decision on how much they will sing. As songs become more familiar, they will gradually join in on verses as well as on the refrain.

With Lyre, Harp
and a Flatpick:
The
Folk
Musician
at
Worship

The difficulty we most often encounter is that verses frequently are more freely worded than refrains. That is, placement of words may be different from verse to verse. If we attempt to teach long sections and several verses, we are likely to tire the people of the song before they have had a chance to experience it. When we use songs designed as hymns (having no refrain), the meter is usually more regular and the people have only to read the words to be able to sing the song.

My personal preference toward antiphonal singing is one of practical experience as well as theoretical reasoning. Very simply, people can comfortably learn two or three refrains and perhaps an acclamation as well; but to ask them to learn three complete hymns would be much more than we ought to burden a congregation with. By singing antiphonally, we have the additional advantage of encouraging listening. If we are well prepared and can sing clearly, people will be encouraged to listen to the words and also be anxious to join when it is their part. We need to offer as many possibilities for listening as we are able because it is such a difficult thing to do and, at the same time, is so important throughout the entire liturgy.

B. THE SOUNDS OF SILENCE . . .

Only on rare occasions are we able to be with people in silence. Usually, we feel uncomfortable, or obliged to "make conversation" to fill up the spaces. In the interest of smooth liturgy we have often eliminated the challenge of silent periods in the course of the celebration. Even in the revised rite, when pauses are called for, we rarely get a chance to experience the silence.

Responsibility for this is usually on the celebrant, but there are instances when we who lead the music have something to say about the length of time between things. We need to consider briefly how we can incorporate the invitations to silence in our role as leaders.

When we begin our work with the people, it is often by a time spent rehearsing songs or explaining what is to take place in that particular celebration. If we want the opening song to actually be a beginning, we have an excellent opportunity for using silence. At the end of the rehearsal (and thanking the people for their attentiveness and, often, patience), we might invite them to a moment of reflection. This period of silence — please make it more than ten or fifteen seconds — allows the congregation to "get out" of the practice session. There is obvious reason for distinguishing the rehearsal and the liturgy, even though they are connected and not to be completely disassociated.

A pause here allows several things. The congregation has a chance to become settled, there is time to gain a bit of anticipation for the service about to begin — and the musical group gets that oft-needed time to rearrange themselves and to turn their own attention toward celebrating the presence of the Lord as they lead the music. (Included parenthetically, because it is anything but our ideal, this short space is available to correct minor emergencies which might have occurred — someone being out of tune, the power for the microphone being turned off, a broken string, a forgotten pick or capo, extra copies of the music, standing in the right place, and so forth. Perish the thought of these things happening, but they do, and we must make the most of our chances to remedy them without causing a major holdup in the movement or the mood of the celebration. There have been times when I have invited people to a moment of silence before we began — and I slipped away to fix something. If we are careful about it, it is possible to do this and not destroy the rapport we have worked so hard to establish, or the confidence which the congregation may now have in us. Let the period of silence be your ace in the hole for unplanned eventualities — and remember another important principle when doing anything in public: *move slowly*, as if everything were under control, and no one will know the difference.)

Acclamations, even though they are led as a bursting-forth, with an element of a "holy cheer", benefit by smooth, quiet movement on our part. During the time immediately prior to the singing, we must be sure not to distract the people from being very able to hear what they are about to respond to. (NB: move

With Lyre, Harp
and a Flatpick:
The
Folk
Musician
at
Worship

like a cat when you are preparing to introduce the Holy, Holy, the Memorial Acclamation or Great Amen!) The people should know beforehand that they will sing certain acclamations; there is no need to remind them by the group's clanging and juggling for position to begin the song. *You might even consider that the short acclamations may be successfully led by a single guitarist-cantor rather than the entire group.* This will permit most effective silence before and after the singing.

A general principle is that if people have an instant to allow themselves to become aware of what their next action will be, they often can be more involved in that action. This also permits the opportunity of noticing what they have just completed. If we are conscious of using silence, and patient enough to allow it sufficient time, there is reason to expect a new level of smoothness and flow in the liturgy. It will need some practice and explanation in order to avoid a hanging uncertainty for the congregation.

C. MUSIC WITH READINGS

We often speak of music as an accompaniment. It sometimes accompanies silence, although more often it attends an action. Another way music can be used effectively is to accompany the **spoken word**. There has yet to be sufficient attention given to helping people respond to the readings of the Word, or to being aware of the presence of Christ in the Word.

The structure of the celebration of the Word has been devised to insure that there has been a hearing of the Word: we are asked to respond. Normally, the Response consists of two sections — a responsorial psalm after the first reading, and an alleluia acclamation after the second in preparation for listening to the Gospel (this acclamation is occasionally repeated after the Gospel). Without a doubt, the response part of the liturgy of the Word provides the musical planner with the best place for imagination and creativity.

The lectionary begins with the first option: the responsorial psalm which has a refrain for the people to recite and then verses for the lector to read. This way is good, but like most "standard" options, it chances monotony setting in after repeated usages. The first way to add music to this part is simply to use instrumental accompaniment throughout the responsorial psalm.

If we want the responder to be more active, we give him a chance to use additonal energy: he may sing part of the psalm. This way of responding has several variations. They may be clearer if we look at them in a list and then reflect on the ways they can best be used:

— **sung refrain, psalm read and accompanied by instrumental music**

— **sung refrain, sung verses, instrumental interlude**

— **sung refrain, a capello verses**

— **sung refrain, musical interlude, repeated refrain**

— **refrain from one of the other songs of the day**

Surely, these have been used many times by your groups, and you will have tried other variations as well. You may find it worthwhile to keep track of what you do each week so that you do not always use the same pattern of response, or forget one of the possible variations all together. The principle here may be best expressed as DO SOMETHING! Don't let this part of the liturgy slip by and be forgotten by the congregation.

We recall that people have heard the Word and that is why they have come to the Eucharist. We want to use the most appropriate section of the liturgy to remind them of this and allow them to be very active as hearers of the Word — at liturgy by symbol, at home by the way they use the Word.

A Few Topics
Also Needing Mention

A. TO ORGANISTS
WHO MAY BE CONCERNED

We are emerging from an era wherein a single musical instrument was authorized and accepted in celebrations of the Church's liturgical worship. It was not *always* so, but the organ has indeed been standard for decades. The folk tradition in church music has grown in popularity — sometimes to the great disappointment of church organists. In some cases this has been due to a narrow insistence on classical forms of music in a worship context — in many other situations, organists have been distressed by folk music because it is done very poorly.

This book upholds the developing folk tradition in liturgical music as a solid dimension of Christian worship — here to stay, in the constantly-evolving style that is its nature. Hardly a "fad", as some would like to believe, the folk tradition is and will be an

With Lyre, Harp
and a Flatpick:
The
Folk
Musician
at
Worship

invigorating force for ever-deeper and more prayerful worship. We folk musicians should always be ready to agree, however, that our style is not the only kind of liturgical music and to affirm the worth and beauty brought to the Church's worship by talented musicians experienced in other styles and traditions. It is especially to church organists, therefore, that these few lines that follow are addressed and dedicated.

Those of you who are organists may have read many of the sections of the book and may have questions about folk music; I hope that by having some guidelines here in print and by discussing our use of guitars and other folk instruments we will be furthering the understanding between people who appreciate different styles of liturgical music. I think the principles we have talked about here are applicable to good liturgy of all kinds — not just folk liturgy or folk music. We have struggled too long arguing over what kind of music is going to be sung at what mass. It is high time for us to occasionally play together in the same celebration, or to know that the use of one kind of music does not exclude the other.

I hope many of the preceding chapters are read by organists and professional musicians as well as folk musicians because I know that many organists and parish music directors have the responsibility of helping the folk musicians. I am sure it is very often the case that the trained musician has a difficult time understanding what the folk musician is trying to do, and I can appreciate that there are differences in taste and styles of music. What seems worthwhile, workable, and useful to one group seems inappropriate to the other group. If, however, we are able to recognize these differences in taste — to grant them their validity — we will surely be able to work together towards good liturgy rather than taking sides against each other.

Erich Sylvester has a story that he often quotes in workshops that we have done together. He has been several places where there is a 9:00 o'clock mass which uses only organ music and a 10:00 o'clock mass which uses only folk music. As the crowds are arriving and leaving in between the masses, no one ever speaks to one another. I find this saddening in terms of the Christian community who, as I understand it, have the responsibility to understand one another and be patient with each other's tastes. Such tolerance will lead toward a healthy diversity as we look for the best way to celebrate the Christian mystery.

If you as a trained musician are working with groups in the parish, I would like to point out a few things that might be helpful from your point of view. The techniques I have outlined are intended to give aid in gaining proficiency on the guitar; they are aimed at helping people who play as they sing, and they additionally provide cohesiveness in arrangement, precision, and an opportunity for good dynamics. The trained musician — organist or music director — surely is aware of the need for good technique and can be helpful as a knowledgeable critic for the folk music group.

The difficulty in most churches has been that the folk music group and the organists have never been able to get together at practices. They have been alienated from each other in terms of taste and have felt that neither wanted to hear what the other

127

With Lyre, Harp
and a Flatpick:
The
Folk
Musician
at
Worship

thought. Anything that was spoken in this atmosphere was not offered as a helpful criticism but as a way of subtly excluding a type of music from the parish celebration.

It has become clear to me over the years in various musical experiences (which range from piano lessons as a child to playing in a marching band to finally concentrating on various folk types of music) that there are enough similarities in music that we need not fight over how we express our faith. Any musician that I have come in contact with has had values and priorities in music basically consisting of clarity, precision, subtlety, accuracy, and proper variations to eliminate monotony — as well as the expressive dynamics which help important parts of the music to stand out. I am reasonably sure that these principles are not substantially different for the New York Philharmonic or Bill Monroe's Blue Grass band. Good music can be done only when all of those aspects are kept in perspective and heeded: so the folk musician and the trained musician need not be at odds.

If there is anything that I hope for in the future of liturgical music it is that those of greater musical experience will be willing to share some of their knowledge with others who are learning or are in a medium, like folk music, which sometimes appears to be very simple.

We spend considerable time talking about criticism and evaluation. If the other musicians of the parish are able to notice things that the folk group needs in order to perform its music better or to be better able to lead the congregation, then surely these other musicians should be willing to share their thoughts with the folk group. But the criticism must be offered with a positive attitude. If the musicians are told that their music is inconsistent or has no taste or that they are basically dumb people anyway, they are not likely to accept the criticism. On the other hand, if a word of encouragement can be added while one points out a problem or a mistake, then criticism will be taken positively and will not be a hindrance for the group nor cause further rift between exponents of different styles of music.

I cannot ask too much of organists except that they be patient with different kinds of musicians. As organists, you've always been directors and sometimes folk groups tend to direct themselves. And too, because of the long struggle many people have engaged in to have folk music permitted in some parishes, there is a tendency to overreact to any comments from organists and choir directors. I hope that any of you who have read through this book will understand more about the folk musician and be able to talk with him in his terms. Please listen to him and consider his taste. If you do so, you will be building a strong bond of tolerance for all kinds of diversity within the parish community.

B. THE PASTOR: A MAN WITH TASTES, TOO — AND THE MAN IN THE MIDDLE!

We should give some consideration now to the other strong force in the parish community, the pastor. Pastors have often been categorized by folk musicians and advocates in such phrases as, "We don't like him," "He won't let us play our guitars," or "We have a good pastor; he lets us have two folk masses a week." Surely, there is more depth to a person than whether or not he encourages or discourages the use of folk music in worship.

129

With Lyre, Harp
and a Flatpick:
The
Folk
Musician
at
Worship

As we mentioned before, an important part of building parish communities is listening to people on their own terms, hearing their real tastes, and knowing what is helpful to them. This is very important when we are interacting with a pastor who may initially be totally uninterested in folk music (perhaps because he has had a bad experience with musicians who were inexperienced or unqualified, or simply because of his own personal preferences in music).

PARISH

PARISH
LITURGY TEAM

We owe pastors, as we owe all of the members of the Christian community, respect for their own tastes but at the same time there is no reason for our not doing everything possible to show them that other people's tastes are also worthwhile. If the pastor of our parish is reluctant to initiate the use of folk music, our best method of gaining his trust in our competance is to be willing and able to demonstrate quality music to him. As we have said over and over, we cannot force someone to like any individual song or style, but, if the song is good, it provides its own invitation. Patience and perserverance are the best encouragements I can give for increasing the use of folk music in your parish. Having many supporters of folk music often is necessary to demonstrate the need for it.

C. THE BISHOP SAID WHAT?

We usually think of the bishops only when they send letters to be read on Sunday or when we see them in our parishes for Confirmation. As they are involved in the complexities of organizing large dioceses, they also make statements which inform us of the local church situation. Among the best statements I have read is the recent publication from the bishops' committee on liturgy entitled *Music in Catholic Worship.* * It is probably the clearest and most concise statement about music and liturgy that has emerged in recent years, and every parish musician or singer should be familiar with it. This statement gives us norms and clarifications concerning use of music. Its outline covers such topics as judging music, specific places in the liturgy for song, ideas about the power of music, and so on. I must admit that I have taken liberally from these guidelines and, although I have not given footnotes, I would like to recognize the value of the statement and acknowledge my use of it.

---

*Published by U.S. Catholic Conference. See p. 181.

With Lyre, Harp
and a Flatpick:
The
Folk
Musician
at
Worship

Each of the major sections of this document has served as a good reminder to me of the things we should keep in mind when we are planning and celebrating. I find them worthy of reflection and hope that the same will be true for you.

The bishops remind us that *"a man is a Christian because through the Christian community he has met Jesus Christ, heard his word in invitation, and responded to him in faith. Christians gather at Mass that they may hear and express their faith again in this assembly, and, by expressing it, renew and deepen it."* This comes about by way of signs and symbols; we are attempting to communicate this response to each other and to God our Father. *"The signs should be simple,"* the bishops say, *"clear and unencumbered . . . if they need to be explained to communicate faith, they will often be watched, rather than celebrated."*

To us musicians, almost a personal remark: *"The quality of joy and enthusiasm which music adds to community cannot be gained in any other way. Music, in addition to expressing texts, can also unveil a dimension of meaning and feeling, a communication of ideas and intuitions which words alone cannot yield."* They go to some length to remind us again of the importance of being critical in order to achieve the best celebrations. We are told to make a threefold judgement: Musical, Liturgical and Pastoral. Over and over again throughout the document, we read about the uniqueness of situations, groups and occasions with a reminder to be attentive to that uniqueness.

We are also given an excellent working summary of the structure of the liturgy. The explanation of the Liturgy of the Word states that *"it is of primary importance that the people hear God's message, digest it with the aid of psalms, silence, and the homily, and respond, involving themselves in the great covenant of love and redemption. All else is secondary.*

With the explanation of the Liturgy of the Eucharist (. . . *a prayer of thanksgiving and sanctification which is the center of the entire celebration . . . in which the whole congregation joins Christ in acknowledging the works of God and offering the Sacrifice . . .)* we have a concise reminder to give support to our usual thoughts on liturgy.

There is a strong section toward the end in which we read: *"Flexibility reigns supreme . . . for the composer and performer alike there is an unprecedented challenge. He must enhance the liturgy with new creations of variety and richness and with those compositions from the time-honored treasury of liturgical music which can still serve today's celebration."* We are reminded over and over, by these words as well as those of the parish communities we work with that we have a serious task to try to do well. This and other sections of *Music in Catholic Worship* give us both challenge and support — the ongoing effort must be made, and it is something which once again raises the question we spoke of at the very beginning of Part Two — what have we gotten ourselves into??? The bishops say much about it; the fullest answer must come from within each of us. We are, I am sure, making progress as long as we are looking at things seriously and keep hearing what is being spoken.

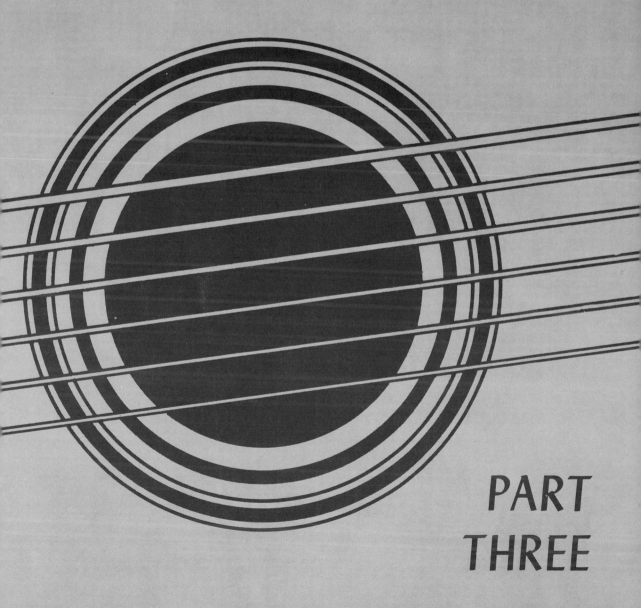

Appendix

PART
THREE

APPENDIX

For Better Playing -
A Lesson or Three

No doubt, in your life as a musician, you have used or at least come in contact with many varied plans or programs which guarantee instant success in learning your instrument. I would rather not attempt to offer another such solution, but in the end it may look like that.

I have looked over many different songs and have also tried to remember ways that most helped me learn to play the guitar. I have a difficult time deciding whether there are only a few licks to learn or whether there are so many that it is impossible to outline them completely. Hopefully, some of the more important guitar techniques described here will give you some direction in your advancement as a musician. I wouldn't expect for you to learn them all in the same length of time that it takes to read these page but, if you were able to try one or two new things each week, you might find that in the course of several months or a year you will have added a great deal to your musical skills.

With Lyre, Harp
and a Flatpick:
The
Folk
Musician
at
Worship

The guitar is a strange instrument. While we have two distinct sections to contend with, that is, the right hand and the left hand, the overall effect is seldom accomplished without proper coordination of the two. Therefore, whenever you learn a new skill (even though it may be concentrated in one hand) be sure to be aware of what is being done with both hands.

As I recall learning to play the guitar, the first thing I did was to become familiar with the names of the notes which the first three or four frets represented. This was helpful to me primarily because of my early experience with the piano. With my piano background, the guitar made sense when I had an idea of why placing my fingers in certain places caused chords to sound.

The following music staff shows the range of basic notes which may be played on the first few frets of the guitar:

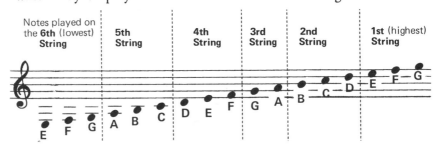

Here is where you find these notes of the scale on the guitar fretboard (neck):

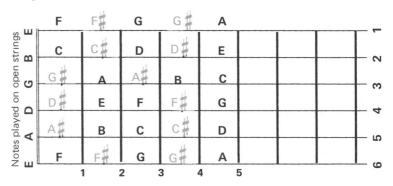

Shown below and on the following pages are examples of songs whose basic melodies can actually be played with only two strings of the guitar. Try the refrain of *Proclaim His Marvelous Deeds*, written by Joe Zsigray. You can do it using just the 2nd and 3rd strings of the guitar:

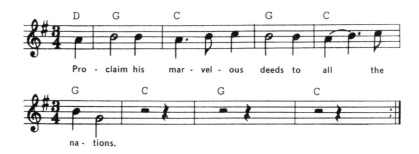

From the Recording and Sheet Music by Joe Zsigray titled BERAKAH. Copyright 1972 by North American Liturgy Resources. All Rights Reserved.

With Lyre, Harp
and a Flatpick:
The
Folk
Musician
at
Worship

You can practice playing a melody using only the 4th and 5th strings with the refrain of *Jesus, In Our Hands* by Joe Wise.

Je - sus, in our hands we a - dore you.

Je - sus, in our flesh we touch your bo - dy sac - red

grown. Je - sus, in this bread we learn to

bake our lives as one. Fill up your bo - dy,

show us the love we've known, show

us the love we've known.

From the Recording and Sheet Music WATCH WITH ME. Copyright 1972 by Joe Wise. All Rights Reserved. Published by North American Liturgy Resources.

You may notice in playing the chords for *Jesus, In Our Hands* that all the notes except the F♯ (4th string, 4th fret) are within the formation of the standard chord patterns. Later on, you will be able to combine the notes and the rhythm for a more expanded accompaniment or possibly for use as an instrumental.

Knowing what notes make up a particular chord may not appeal to you, but such knowledge is necessary when you wish to learn new songs from printed music. Moreover, we usually need all the help we can get to understand some of the logic of the guitar neck — believe it or not, there is more than random arrangement to the notes! As you become somewhat familiar with the arrangement of notes, you will find that you can use your knowledge of the basic chord patterns for greater diversity of playing.

For better playing:
Chords
are
made of
NOTES!

FREEING YOUR FINGERS — A FIRST STEP

Because most of us started on the guitar by learning patterns which produced basic chords, we often have (unintentionally) locked ourselves into a limited type of playing. There are ways, however, through which we can immediately vary what we do and begin to develop "digital independence." That is to say, the fingers of our left hand can do much more than form chords!

For example, the first technique which most folk-style guitar manuals offer to the student is the age old technique of **hammering-on**. The technique involves raising one or other finger while remaining within the basic chord pattern. I suspect someone discovered this technique when intending to readjust his grip on the guitar and found that the two notes together added something to the simple chord which he was playing. By using the hammering-on technique, we can accomplish two things: Immediately, we add something to the music, and we gain a skill with the left hand.

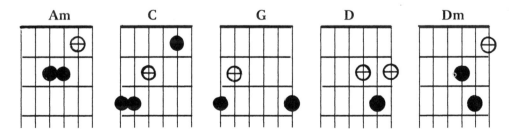

(The ⊕ indicates notes to be hammered-on; these are examples only — experiment with other notes. There are many possibilities.)

141

With Lyre, Harp
and a Flatpick:
The
Folk
Musician
at
Worship

When you are practicing or using a hammering technique, instead of returning to the same string, try playing some other note that is within your reach (See chart). An example of this would be in a standard C chord fingering. Raising the middle finger from the E note (second fret, 4th string), and instead of returning it immediately to that E note, play an A which requires only that you strike the second fret of the 3rd string. Experimentation with this exercise will permit you to find that many harmonic notes are within your reach in almost any chord formation. What we would hope to accomplish from assorted hammering practices and other exercises is a gradual freeing of the left hand to play a wider variety of notes.

Try these hammering exercises using your normal C-G-D chord patterns.

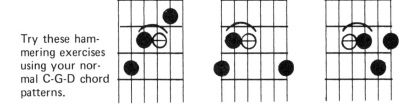

These hammering exercises also help us begin to hear variations on chords which eventually can add a great deal to the beauty of the music. By simply reversing the hammering-on technique, we arrive at another which is most profoundly termed **pulling-off**. As you are playing a certain chord pattern, add a little more pressure to a given string and, moving your finger in either direction, quickly lift it from the string. A new note will be sounded. A good beginning practice on this technique would be with a D chord formation. Here the middle finger of the left hand can pull the E string and give the extra note to the chord. You will find that this technique can often be combined with hammering for pleasant addition of syncopation to the strum or picking pattern you may be using.

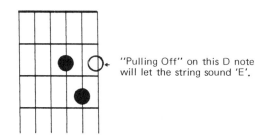

"Pulling Off" on this D note will let the string sound 'E'.

For better playing:

Freeing
your
fingers:
a first
step

As we mentioned, right and left hand activities need to be coordinated. If you wish to increase the skill of your right hand, you might pick the individual string which the left hand is hammering-on or pulling-off. The best developed folk music accompaniment can be accomplished by accurate use of the flat pick or picking style in these simple variations in the left hand.

When we shift consideration to the right hand, we have several alternatives. These range from strumming all the strings to strumming a few of the strings to combining picking individual strings with strumming a few strings to finger picking. If we hope to accomplish anything more sophisticated than the washboard effect (playing all the strings all the time on every chord), we must be aware that individual attention to the strings with the right hand is as important as the attention given to individual strings in the left hand. Every note played adds either harmony or dissonance to a chord. Best music is achieved when we choose which harmonies and dissonances are present.

The simplest way to avoid dissonances which are undesired is not to play open strings which are outside the chord formation or which give a wrong emphasis. By playing strings slowly when you are learning a new chord, you can notice which open strings are desireable, and which are not. You may then practice picking notes accordingly.

In the examples below, "X" indicates the open string is not played, while "O" indicates an open string to be played.

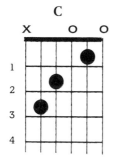
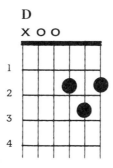
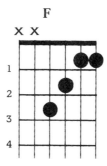

143

With Lyre, Harp
and a Flatpick:
The
Folk
Musician
at
Worship

BASS NOTES

The right hand has the task of defining rhythm and the important notes of any chord. We must, therefore, have some knowledge of which strings go best with which chords. Hopefully, when you learned chords, you learned the primary bass note of that chord. This bass note, coupled with a secondary bass note, will permit you to give clear bass accompaniment as well as rhythm to your playing. These bass notes are extremely important and their presence should be made known in whatever style of playing we use.

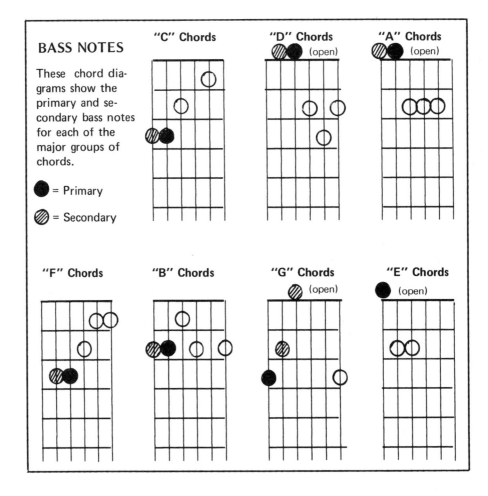

Through the suggestions, illustrations and examples in this section, I wish to help you learn how to make strumming much more than a boring activity which we do for lack of anything better. With even the simple techniques shown, we can indeed have something much better than the washboard strum which has given folk music a black eye in so many churches. The right hand can become as active as the left and actually cause the instrument to be able to speak.

If you are willing to practice the bass notes for each chord until you can play them consistently and with accurate rhythm, I would guarantee that you would be a significantly-improving guitarist. Give yourself ten minutes a day on this style of flat-picking — and listen to what happens!

The following adaptations of music staff lines depict the general pattern for simple exercises you can do to help you incorporate alternating bass notes into your strums. The first is a simple 2/4 rhythm and the second is 3/4, the familiar waltz tempo ("ONE-two-three...")

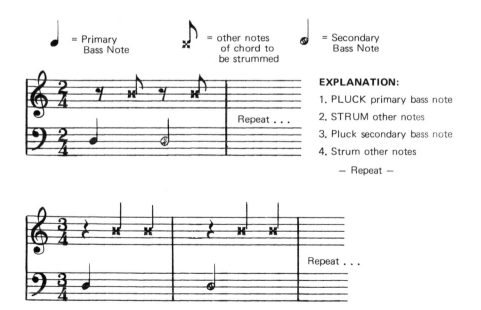

= Primary Bass Note

= other notes of chord to be strummed

= Secondary Bass Note

EXPLANATION:

1. PLUCK primary bass note
2. STRUM other notes
3. Pluck secondary bass note
4. Strum other notes

— Repeat —

Repeat . . .

Repeat . . .

With Lyre, Harp
and a Flatpick:
The
Folk
Musician
at
Worship

It is good to do these exercises with related groups of chords. For example:

$$C - F - G$$
$$G - C - D$$
$$E - A - B^7 \quad \text{etc.}$$

Getting used to changing the bass notes for different chords is important, especially when you later learn to add "runs."

Stay With Me by Erich Sylvester is a good example of a popular liturgical song in 3/4 time. You might like to practice your bass notes using the refrain:

REFRAIN:

Walk with me, talk with me,

tell me a - bout all the good things you've done;

stay with me, pray with me,

leave all your blues in your shoes at the

door. *(guitar)* *to verse*

BASS "RUNS"

Once you become comfortable with the principle of accenting bass notes, your imagination is the only limit to the notes you can play. When you practice these notes, practice them both with flatpick style and finger-pick style; each will allow greater variety and freedom in your playing.

The clearest version of bass note accents is in normal country music accompaniment. If you have ever listened to Blue Grass music, I'm sure you have noticed the strong bass accompaniment performed by the guitar player of the group. While most of these songs have only three or four chords, the guitarist will be constantly playing the important bass notes and runs between the chords. We will illustrate several examples of these bass runs and give some exercises you might like to work on. They will enable you to connect the chords together and eliminate "empty spaces."

In the Key of G: The first run you might try can be from G to E-minor. The bass notes are **G, F♯** and **E**, and the positions are shown in the following photos and chording diagrams:

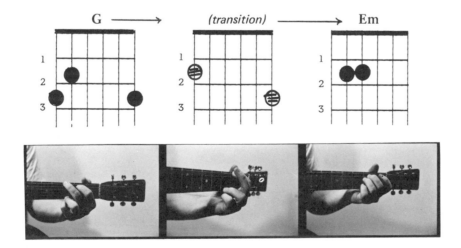

147

With Lyre, Harp
and a Flatpick:
The
Folk
Musician
at
Worship

The run from G to Em can, of course, be reversed from Em back to G.

When moving from G to C, a possible run looks like this:

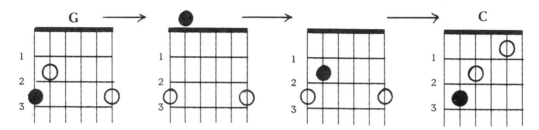

(I might add that this one works best if the G chord is fingered with the 2nd, 3rd and 4th fingers. This allows a smooth shift to the C chord and back.)

Another important chord in the key of G is "D." A run from G to D can be done as shown below:

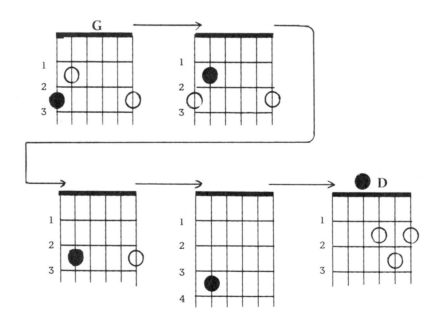

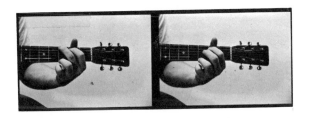

The run from
G to D.

> When practicing runs, be aware that
> the STRUM CAN BE BROKEN —
> that is, omit the brushing across all
> the strings while playing the notes of
> the run. Be sure to do this with
> proper rhythm.

Offered below are runs for several other chords frequently
played together:

C to F —   C chord - notes D and E on 4th string - F chord

D to G —   D chord - notes E and F$\sharp$ on 1st string - G chord

A to D —   A chord - notes B and C$\sharp$ on 5th string - D chord

D to A —   D chord - notes C$\sharp$ and B on 5th string - A chord

E to A —   E chord - notes F$\sharp$ and G$\sharp$ on 6th string - A chord

With Lyre, Harp
and a Flatpick:
The
Folk
Musician
at
Worship

CHORD PROGRESSIONS

As we play many songs we become familiar with standard progressions of the chords (**C —Am — F — G7; C—Em—F—G7; C—F—C—G, etc.**). To help ourselves remain fresh, we can concentrate on accenting the descending bass notes of those progressions. It only takes a minimal switch to bring out this movement in a song. For example:

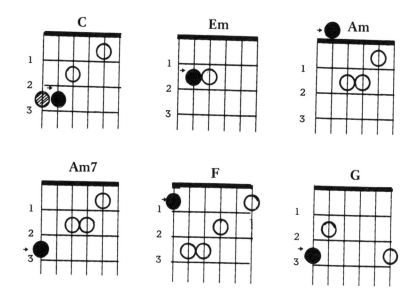

Play these chords in sequence several times and LISTEN to the descending movement of the bass notes.

With the basic principles of chord progression in mind, I used the familiar combination of **C—F** with one variation and an ending of **D9** as the foundation for a song I wrote called *From an Indirect Love.* I offer this progression here for you to try — as an additional way of freeing your fingers to play new positions (but based on familiar ones!):

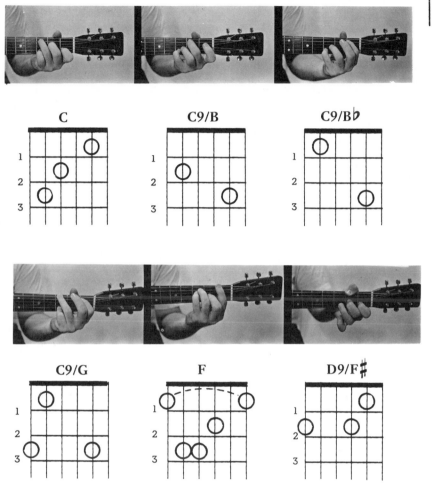

C

C9/B

C9/B♭

C9/G

F

D9/F♯

Yes, you **CAN** play this progression — don't be intimidated by the fancy chord names! What I hope you will see is that these are very close to the chord forms we use every day. I hope, of course, that you like the sound of the progression; more importantly, I do hope you will practice stretching your use of chords to include these harmonic variations. From the ones shown here as examples, you may go on to discover your own.

For improving what we do in another common key, we can look at a very basic progression for **D**:

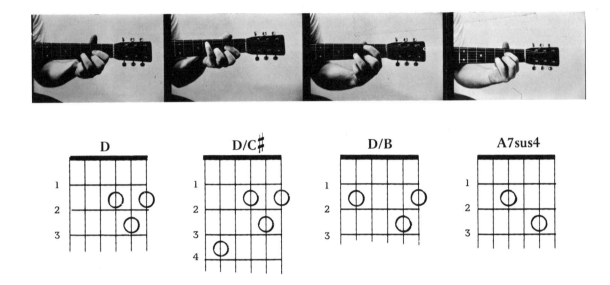

D	D/C♯	D/B	A7sus4

THE WONDERS OF "D - TUNING"

While we are working in the key of D, we can also spend time considering a very helpful technique for playing in that key. The "something extra" for your guitar called "D-tuning" is accomplished by simply lowering the bass E (6th) string to D. Play your normal D chord pattern and listen to the new richness of a complete open and full D chord. On other chords played in the key of D, a few fingering variations are called for, but they are certainly worth it!

As shown on the following page, all that is necessary is to "add" two frets to wherever you normally finger the E-string. The finest use I have had for this technique is with Bob Dylan's *I Shall Be Released*, a simple song which merely moves from the D to Em7 to F♯m7 back to Em7 and finally to D.

  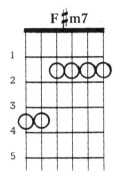 

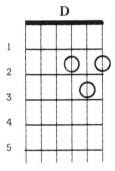 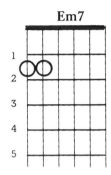

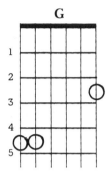

D   **Em7**   **F#m7**   **G**

TEMPO — NO LIMIT TO STYLE!

Back to the RIGHT hand for a moment! With even the simplest of rhythms, our playing need never become monotonous. There are several variations which can be used within each rhythm pattern. For instance, the standard 4/4 tempo can be played in any of the following ways:

              — a complete strum
              — bass note with strum
              — bass note with arpeggio
              — bass with muffled strum
              — bass note(s) with no strum

Remember: you can use several of these patterns within a song as well as using one of them as your style for a particular song.

Similarly, variations may also be learned for finger-picking styles. These might include alternating bass and treble notes, picking bass notes and two or three other notes together, or playing a bass note and lightly strumming with the backs of your fingernails.

153

With Lyre, Harp
and a Flatpick:
The
Folk
Musician
at
Worship

If you will take the time to learn these, you will quickly notice that you have eight variations for the same 4/4 rhythm. To strengthen your playing, learn each of these and practice them with your favorite songs. If you can play any song combining several variations, you will be well on your way to creating excellent musical accompaniment which will remain fresh for the congregation.

* * * INTERLUDE * * *

All the various suggestions offered in this Appendix for improvement of both right hand and left hand technique are within the grasp of anyone who has already been working with the basic folk chord patterns and simple rhythmic strums. Again let me emphasize that these pages are not intended to be a self-contained complete "course." Rather, we are highlighting certain areas for possible improvement which experience has shown to be the best "next moves" for average folk guitarists working with liturgical music. You can indeed learn new "tricks" by working directly with the examples we offer — but never hesitate to pursue these techniques deeper through more complete self-study courses, lessons, or working with a more experienced guitarist.

And practice . . .

ALLELUIA, PRAISE TO THE LORD!

With Lyre, Harp
and a Flatpick:
The
Folk
Musician
at
Worship

EVER SEEN A GUITAR
WITH JUST FOUR FRETS ?

If you're ready to extend your familiarity with the instrument itself, we may begin by discovering that there are also notes to be played above the fourth fret. Learning a few variations on the basic chords which can be played "down there" (up there?) will increase your understanding of the logic of the guitar — and add some fresh sounds to your playing!

For example, when I wrote *Alleluia, Praise to the Lord* I was experimenting in the key of D. I knew that an inversion of the D chord existed on the fifth fret. By playing part of the inversion, the D chord remained and by sliding that same position down two frets I discovered a variation on a C chord. So, while many people have been initially confused by the accompaniment to that song, they have quickly learned it by the addition of one new pattern (see illustration).

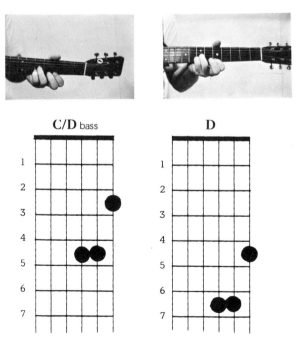

These variations are most effective when used with D-tuning (as explained on p. 152). After understanding the principles involved, you may begin to find your own chord inversions. If you are not already familiar with the guitar neck, you might find it interesting to practice locating chords in different positions, all of them being based on the first patterns you learned. As illustrated below, for example, the fingering for the basic C chord can also be used to play the E and A chords, the E fingering can play A and C, and so forth:

For better playing:
The neck is more than four frets long!

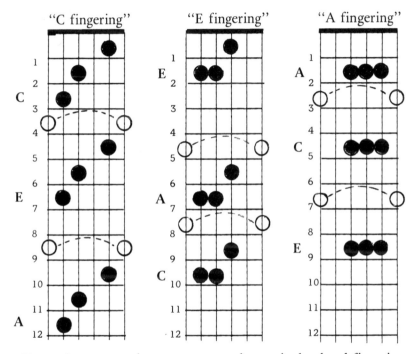

From these examples you can see that a single chord-fingering pattern can produce a number of different chords, depending on where it is played — and that an individual chord can be played in several different ways. The logical pattern here also demonstrates how a number of other chords are formed: the normal E chord moved up 2 frets becomes F♯ , and Am moved up 2 frets becomes the Bm chord.

Understanding and using chord inversions permits you to create varities for the introductions and endings of songs.

157

With Lyre, Harp
and a Flatpick:

The
Folk
Musician
at
Worship

What we have here is the opportunity to play a chord almost anywhere we choose! It is simply a matter of counting frets. For example, take the E-position and count up to the 8th fret; you will go E - F - F♯ - G - G♯ - A - A♯ - B - C — your fingers keep the same pattern, but now you have a new chord. And — stopping on any fret along the way gives that respective chord. (Such chords may be partially fingered, as most people finger an F chord, or completely fingered if you can bar the chord). Try the same with an Am chord — where is Dm? With some time and practice, you will find that you seldom need a chord chart to find any version of any chord.

When we use these variations, we discover that we are better able to create different *moods* on the guitar.

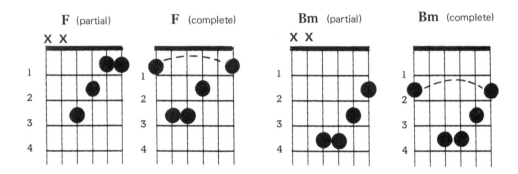

Note: **"X"** = not played.

PLAY IT WITH FEELING!

Imaginative new positions for familiar chords does indeed do much to set the stage for the mood of a song. Very often, by playing a simple chord like Em or G in a different position, we are able to make the difference between lightness and intensity for a song.

Of course, it will be the variations we create with our RIGHT hand that will put the mood across!

When we use these variations we discover that we are better able to create different moods on the guitar. We can play very mellow yet distinct notes by giving special attention to the way we pick the strings. When you have an opportunity, consider the many different moods you can express with your guitar. Take the time to use just one string and try to play a single note with differing moods attached. When you know the different tones that are available, you will be able to arrange them into the accompaniment and the music will therefore be more expressive. This exercise can be done with either one string or two or all of them. You may be surprised at how many different sounds can be made by those six strings. The more you familiarize yourself with these sounds the better able you will be to make the instrument say exactly what you wish.

For better playing:
Play it with feeling!

See if you are able to play "moods" on your guitar. Your options in how you play include the following:

* using a pick, or your fingers

* playing near the bridge or away

* "hard" sounds or soft ones

* fast or slow

* hesitantly or aggressively

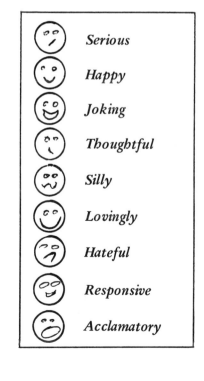

Serious

Happy

Joking

Thoughtful

Silly

Lovingly

Hateful

Responsive

Acclamatory

With Lyre, Harp
and a Flatpick:
The
Folk
Musician
at
Worship

SCALES REVISITED

To further improve your playing, you may wish to practice scales. Traditionally the most agonizing type of exercise, they nevertheless strengthen the hands and make the playing more versatile and precise. I will illustrate one method of scales which you may begin with. There are other ways you can learn and, if you become very serious about it, you may wish to consult André Segovia's Diatonic and Minor Scales.

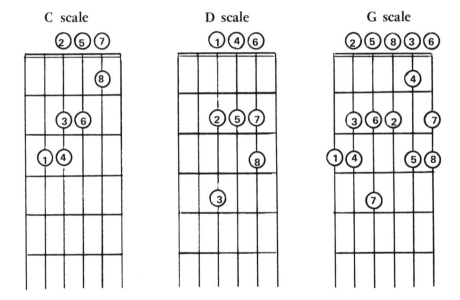

C scale   D scale   G scale

To practice, begin with the lowest (1) and proceed to the highest note (8) marked on the diagram. The principle for finger positioning is to allow one finger for each fret — so that you will be using 1, 2 and 3 most frequently.

Notice how these scale notes fit into the chord patterns you have learned. (You might go back now and try playing *Jesus, In Our Hands.*)

INSTRUMENTALS, IMPROVISATION . . .

When the instrumental accompaniment for a song is to be emphasized, or when we are actually playing an instrumental, we need to consider how the music is to be arranged. First, of course, we must work out ways to bring out the meaning and mood of a song. You've tried conveying specific "moods" with the guitar. It is possible that the average folk style accompaniment can produce excellent instrumental music without the need for complicated patterns. Simple following the chord structure of a song will often make for a good instrumental.

If you have two guitarists, playing in different keys and using a capo will bring out new harmonies. Or, you may easily create instrumental music by improvising on the important notes of a key combined with chord accompaniment. Be sure to try this — you and your partner will find yourselves making fresh new sounds and also improving your skills. Joe Zsigray's song *If We Love One Another* is arranged below for practice with two guitars.

Guitar A (open) — (C) (Em) (Dm) (G7)
Guitar B (capo 5th fret) — G Bm Am D7

If we love one a - no — ther,

(C) (Em) (Dm) (G7)
G Bm Am D7

God will live in us in per - fect love.

(C) (Em) (Dm) (G7)
G Bm Am D7

If we love one a — no — ther,

(C) (G7) (C) (G7)
G D7 G D7

we will live in the love of God.

161

With Lyre, Harp
and a Flatpick:
The
Folk
Musician
at
Worship

One of my friends who is a rock musician has shown me patterns which are useful for this type of improvisation. They are formed around basic blues patterns and can easily be learned. After you have learned one, you will be able to move to many different positions on the guitar to accomodate almost any key. The two examples which I most frequently use are built around formations of the key of E and the key of C. If you will take the illustration below and practice it while someone else is playing chords, you will soon notice how these harmonies fit together.

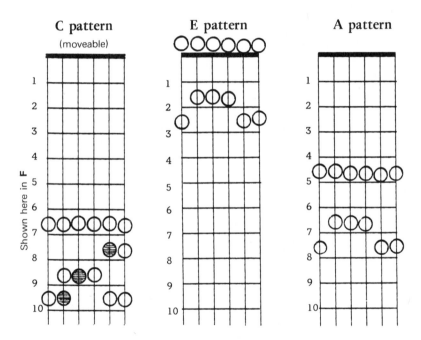

These patterns show the groups of notes which can be played ad lib in simple improvisation. The first diagram shows the pattern for "C" moved up 7 frets to be applied to a song played in the key of "G". (The shaded notes indicate the C-chord fingering pattern.) You may wish to use a capo on the 7th fret to play this improvisation. For practice, have someone play a familiar song in the key of G while you experiment with random playing of the pattern shown. Once you gain confidence playing in these patterns, you can shift to any key desired.

Using this pattern, you will begin to gain confidence and dexterity in single note playing. Because of the random usefulness of these patterns, any of the notes will be harmonic. Later, you will be able to play portions of melodies to go along with the chording of a song. In the beginning you might try this kind of arrangement for introductions or musical interludes. Later, when you gain more expertise, you might play complete instrumental songs. I would hope that this increased knowledge of the guitar will lead you to continued curiosity, and a desire to work towards greater understanding of the instrument.

A final advantage to this improvisational type of playing is that we have a built-in opportunity to write songs. By paying close attention to improvisations and, believe it or not, the mistakes we make, we will discover notes and patterns which may develop into our own music.

With Lyre, Harp
and a Flatpick:
The
Folk
Musician
at
Worship

I recall an afternoon at a retreat several months ago when things were rather quiet and I had the opportunity to sit with the guitar and play. I began playing a familiar series of chords. At one point my fingers slipped from the E string. The note stood out and I liked it. After playing it several more times, I found that I had created the accompaniment for a song, *Lord Have Mercy on Us All.* You will find an illustration of this "mistake" below. It is by hearing notes with which we are unfamiliar that we are able to discover new musical possibilities, even if they are accidents!

So, if you have a mind to experiment, take your guitar and play. Play whatever note or chord that occurs to you. Often it will be a song you are familiar with, but sometimes you will move to melodies or chords which are very different. As this musical roaming takes place, be attentive to what patterns you are playing and capture those new melodies as they occur. You may discover that you have written a song!

The licks presented here are among the most important I have learned. Some you may know already and use with great ease. Others you may find will take some time. I assure you that all of them are learnable and, if taken in small sections, can eventually be combined into useful and impressive accompaniment patterns.

Most of us as musicians rely on the instruments we play chiefly as a means to accompany our singing. We work for guitar arrangements which we can play comfortably while we sing and which help bring the music to life. Because we usually use the instrument with accompaniment in mind, we often do not think of its use alone. But we **can** invent musical arrangements which either aid our singing or may be played as instrumentals at various times in services.

If you have just a bit of fanaticism within you, you will be willing to keep learning. I presume at least a minimal quantity of such determination in all guitar pickers; otherwise you never would have survived the initial sore fingers required when you first learned. Good luck with these suggestions and I encourage you to make up a few more. There are many waiting to be discovered within your fingers and the guitar.

With Lyre, Harp
and a Flatpick:
The
Folk
Musician
at
Worship

TO PLAY IN BETTER KEYS

We all know we can use a capo to raise the voice range of a song. However, it is worth a little study and practice to become able to change the chording of a song to a different and hopefully more playable and singable key.

The basic principle is this: to transpose a song, raise or lower every note and every chord by the *same* number of "intervals." ("Intervals", if the term is new to you, are simply the numbering system for the eight notes of any major scale. Remembering that each fret on the guitar is a half-step of a scale, the guitarist knows that the distance between each note is a full step or two frets — except between the 3rd and 4th and the 7th and 8th notes, which are half-steps or one fret. For instance, C to D is a full step, with E to F being a half step. Because intervals are the foundation for chord formations, you will find a brief study of them in a simple music theory book such as Book III of the **Don Schenk Method for Guitar** both enlightening and concretely helpful.)

The chart on page 167 illustrates the relationships of chords in a number of different keys and can be used as a reference guide for transposing the chords of a song. Example: for a song which uses the chords of **C - F - G - Em**, the corresponding chords in the key of **G** would be **G - C - D - Bm**. (In using this chart, add "m", "7th", "diminished" and so forth to the major form of the chord.)

A song in the key of **E♭** might contain **E♭ - Gm - B♭ - C**. A more playable key on the guitar might be **D**. Looking at the chart, we go down one key and find that **D - F♯m - A - B** are the corresponding chords. This makes the chords much easier to play, but now the pitch or range for singing might be too low! Simply use the capo to raise the key — one fret for each key to be made up.

NOW — there's no reason to be scared away by a good song whose chords seem complicated. Using transposition and the capo, you can easily play the song with more familiar chord patterns, and still be in a comfortable voice range!

GUIDE TO TRANSPOSING CHORDS IN CHANGING KEYS

Remember: "C" can also represent Cm, C6, C7, Cmaj7, Co, C+, Cm7, C9, Cmaj9, C7sus4, C11, C13, Cm6 and so forth. Be sure to add these designations to the principal form of the new chord you have found in transposing.

Key of C	D	E	F	G	A	B	C
Key of C♯	D♯	F	F♯	G♯	A♯	C	C♯
Key of D	E	F♯	G	A	B	C♯	D
Key of E♭	F	G	A♭	B♭	C	D	E♭
Key of E	F♯	G♯	A	B	C♯	D♯	E
Key of F	G	A	B♭	C	D	E	F
Key of F♯	G♯	A♯	B	C♯	D♯	F	F♯
Key of G	A	B	C	D	E	F♯	G
Key of A♭	B♭	C	D♭	E♭	F	G	A♭
Key of A	B	C♯	D	E	F♯	G♯	A
Key of B♭	C	D	E♭	F	G	A	B♭
Key of B	C♯	D♯	E	F♯	G♯	A♯	B

NOTE: It may be necessary to use a capo to obtain proper voice range for the new set of chords.

With Lyre, Harp
and a Flatpick:

The
Folk
Musician
at
Worship

CHOOSING
AND CARING FOR
YOUR GUITAR

Some suggestions for your next (or your
first) personal guitar—and for church groups
who provide instruments for their regular
musicians . . .

A good guitar cannot make up for poor playing, but a bad
guitar is a frustrating stumbling block to serious learning. Whether
you are choosing a guitar for yourself or responsible for providing
proper instruments for use in your church's liturgical program,
there are a few do's and don'ts I would like to share with you.

Guitars come in every range of price and quality imaginable.
You must decide how much you are able and willing to spend and
how demanding you are of quality. The $300-$1000 instruments
preferred by most experienced guitarists are not necessary — but
anybody serious about learning and playing deserves something
better than the $29.95 discount store special, even though it looks
as good as any other guitar.

In choosing a guitar, you are concerned with three things:

   1) **Tone quality**
   2) **Precision in construction**
   3) **Ease of playing**

Before we proceed, let's settle on the fact that worthwhile
guitars sufficiently meeting the above criteria will have list selling
prices of $85 to $175. While sums in this range might be more
than you might like to spend at one time, it would be best to use
a borrowed instrument while you arrange to invest in an instrument
worth owning. In considering the cost, remember that a good
guitar can last many, many years!

You will not be able to do much to change the sound of a
guitar once you own it, so be careful in your selection. LISTEN to

sound, both individual notes and full chords. Choose on the basis of clarity and good tonal qualities. If you are inexperienced, do not hesitate to ask for help.

Cheaper guitars generally lack the precision and quality construction that are so important for a guitar which is actually going to be played. One of the most frustrating characteristics of cheap guitars is to be constantly out of tune because of looseness in the tuning screws. Sloppy fret spacing will show up especially when you use a capo.

How does it play? Poor guitars require considerable strain in the left hand when forming chords — the strings are too high over the neck to compensate for the probability that the neck will warp or is not true to begin with. Finger a variety of chord patterns on the guitars you try out. The action should be close and the neck must be arrow straight. (If one particular instrument has especially good tone but seems to have just a little too much space between the strings and the neck, some adjustment of the spacing is possible by a qualified specialist.)

My personal choice of guitars is my Martin D-28 which was made in 1954. This company's quality has continued over the years — though some do say to be careful with the very newest ones. This guitar is a 6-string (steel) flat-top model, and I chose it because of power and clarity. Steel generally gives an advantage over nylon strings unless you have an **exceptional** sound system.

It is difficult to recommend company names, because guitars all vary according to when they were made. As a rule, they improve with age! If you are buying a new instrument in the price range suggested, check the Yamaha models and others of Japanese manufacture being marketed by leading American firms. Such instruments have proven quite satisfactory. Excellent guitars are, of course, made in this country and are usually more expensive.

Again I urge you to be willing to spend in at least a medium price range when you are ready to buy. Low quality instruments are difficult to tune accurately, will rarely stay tuned, and lack distinctness in sound. There is seldom hope for playing bar chords,

169

With Lyre, Harp
and a Flatpick:
The
Folk
Musician
at
Worship

hammering or slides, which severely limits the potential of your playing. A better instrument not only meets the essential qualifications of a guitar but can also have the effect of making you **want** to play more often and to try new things. I have always found that to be the case.

If you are willing to include **patience** with a desire to save money, you can search for a good second-hand instrument. I personally would prefer buying a guitar which has had the chance to age and have the bugs worked out. Again — be sure to get a more experienced guitarist to help you in your choice if you do not feel confident in doing it alone.

TAKING CARE OF IT . . .

Obviously a guitar should be handled gently. Be willing to spend those few extra dollars on a case, a great aid to preventing nicks, cracks and collecting dust. Don't leave it in your car in extremes of hot or cold (or with the car unlocked!). You may return to find it in pieces or warped beyond repair. Keep it clean — this actually does make it easier to play in addition to protecting the finish. However, do not go wild with polishes and so forth; very little, if any, is needed.

The other important variable is the strings. **No guitar can deliver its potential once the strings have died!** This is about the only way to describe what happens to guitar strings after a while. They tarnish, collect oil and dirt, and lose their tension. It then becomes impossible for them to vibrate clearly.

If you play every day, change strings about once every four to six weeks. If you only play occasionally, they may last longer.

You will know by the *thud* which dead strings make! (If you want extra life from strings or have an emergency, it is possible to renew them a bit by taking them off the guitar and placing them in a pan of water with a strong dose of household cleaner. Boil them a bit and then go over them with a steel wool pad and then dry them. It makes a remarkable difference — for a while!)

Guitar strings are selected according to gauge and material. If in doubt, get advice. The typical standard-size guitar normally is best with medium-gauge bronze strings. Pay attention to how the strings sound.

Good instrument — good care — good strings. You won't be sorry!

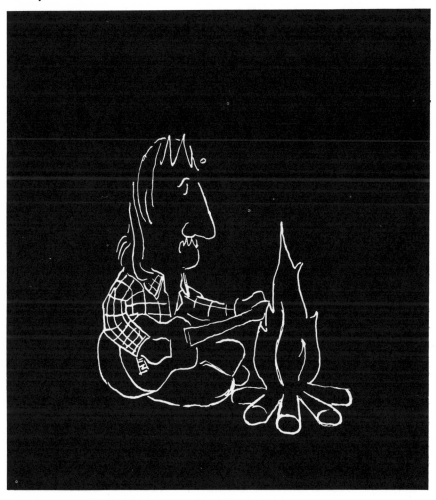

Note: While the illustration captures one of those rare and beautiful moments in the life of a guitarist, I should warn you that playing a guitar near a campfire on a cold starry night is very dangerous for the guitar! The front roasts, the back freezes, and the result is more splinters for the fire!

With Lyre, Harp
and a Flatpick:
The
Folk
Musician
at
Worship

PICKERS, etc.

I am often accused of using a strange vocabulary which includes words like **pickers** and **licks**. I like these words because I have learned them from musicians who are very close to the roots of folk music — people who have learned music from their childhood in the mountains or in other places where truly authentic American folk music is still found. Too often we are more than willing to use styles of music which we call folk and which we know are as old as the American tradition; yet, when someone says "country music," we tend to snicker. Because I have been privileged to gain much from old-time musicians, I like to keep my music and my vocabulary closely tied to them.

If we are happy with the roots of the music we use to celebrate with, we will be willing to give an ear to some of its developments. It seems unfair to take the part of the tradition we like and put down other parts we don't quite understand. If you really want to gain a perspective on American folk music, take the time to attend a folk festival or Blue Grass festival when one is in your neighborhood. I believe you will enjoy it and have an opportunity to learn a great deal about performing music.

Rather Than a Conclusion

Of all the sections of the book, none has been so difficult as attempting to bring things together and conclude. I have let it rest, been away from it and thought more, and started several times — still there remained the difficulty of actually ending. It seems there should be something either profound or clever which would somehow convince both you and me that there has now been enough said on our subject.

If I wait much longer, however, publication will never take place; so, instead of ending, I will take this opportunity to add a few thoughts — with a hope that we can continue to learn and understand our music, liturgy, and our service to the people of God. Since this learning cannot stop, neither must our reflection on and improvement of what we offer. In this way, we may avoid becoming definitive in any of our attitudes (save, perhaps, dynamism) toward the ministry of music.

Several things come to mind. At this point I see them as personal ideals, but offer them in hope that we will be working together on many of them.

With Lyre, Harp
and a Flatpick:
The
Folk
Musician
at
Worship

I wish to notice regularly how I worship as a musician, attempting to avoid becoming mechanistic and detached from those with whom I celebrate and pray. This requires effort at being involved in — and forming — a unified worshipping community; and, therefore, concentration on praying better with people.

I wish to understand the Gospel — to know what we are celebrating. Vagueness is often annoying. And, the more I seem to be learning, the more complex things seem to become. Nevertheless, I want to grow in the ability to understand and communicate our faith and the ways we celebrate it to those who also search for liturgy which is genuinely worship.

The message of the Gospel is a revelation which offers us direction and light. I hope to better see the simpleness of its message which lies within the complex and paradoxical appearance. When this can happen, we can, as we sing, come closer to being born again and continuing that birth to further heights. Hopefully, our collective attention to better liturgy will bring this newness of life to each of us.

I am haunted by many other questions: how are we able to be more involved members of the Christian community both on Sunday and on our streets? Does the celebrating end with the last song? When we change our liturgy, must we not also change our lives? Jesus spoke very strongly concerning worship and living (and in no uncertain terms to those who worshipped loudly and ignored their brothers). We cannot pray in isolation; our communities need our involvement and response if we are to live as Christ has challenged us. How unfortunate that we cannot merely sing well and expect the kingdom to unfold before us!

It may be, however, that we will lead music best and have more to celebrate when we are working seriously at *being* Christian. Though it would be nice to escape, there is the ever-present paradox of the Gospel — it is in dying that we live and in giving away what we have (as musicians or whoever) that we are most involved and, therefore, most helpful to our congregations. Our participation in liturgy is but one aspect of our membership in the Christian community, one which should be a reflection of our usual living. Our attention to the needs of family, friends, co-workers, the sick, the poor, and strangers   is among the other areas which determine our membership and whether we are serious about it.

As I reflect on these questions there arises still another conclusion as well as an ideal: I wish to be more patient . . . as well as less! This encourages me to have an honest understanding of differences of experiences in the hope of reconciling many of the polarities which exist in our parishes. There is the reminder in Scripture that if there is something wrong between myself and my brother, I must leave my gift at the altar and go be reconciled first. This reconciliation can only take place by being willing to see other peoples' priorities and interests.

When done in a spirit of understanding, meekness, and kind - ness, reconciliation is formative as well as challenging, for it is often difficult to wait for someone and understand him and act with honesty and care at the same time. Conflicting as it seems, I believe we can love that way and bring about change — especially if we are less patient with our own slowness to learn, and dishon- esty which is often disguised as diplomacy (when it is often rooted in fear of speaking what I believe to be the truth).

Finally, and perhaps the most difficult of all — to risk that the Lord and others will hear if I dare to speak with faith, hope and love; to proclaim the works of God, to give Him thanks, and to further the realization and bringing about of the Kingdom we know in the meeting and believing of Jesus Christ; to love more and continue believing that what I have already seen is an indi- cation of things to come. Those of you whom I know enable me to continue believing it IS happening!

With Lyre, Harp
and a Flatpick:
The
Folk
Musician
at
Worship

Some Additional Help

*Following is a selected collection of books and other resources
which could be part of the library of the folk musician serious
about serving the Church's liturgical needs and developing his or her
abilities and sensitivities.*

Pete Seeger
THE INCOMPLEAT FOLKSINGER
(New York: Simon & Schuster, 1972) 596 pp. $12.50

Pete Seeger, a father and a prophet of the "folk revival" appears to have created THE book for today's folksingers. Journeying from the roots through to
the present and future of folk music, he brings it all together in a relaxed and
free style which in itself shows a lot of what "folk" is all about. He speaks of
ways of singing with and for people, of the instruments, of making new songs,
and of styles, standards and responsibilities in our living heritage of homemade
music. He views the world that music lives in: races and racism, money and
commercial music, patriotism, protest, and language. The book has wit, vision,
and solid practical helpfulness. The printed text is pleasantly arranged, com-
plemented with photos, sketches, helpful diagrams and, of course, songs.

Rev. James Dallen
WORSHIP IN A NEW WORLD
(Cincinnati: North American Liturgy Resources, 1972) $1.95

This is the best "first" book for acquainting the lay person with the spirit and
purpose of the new Order of Mass. The explanations are unusually clear and
readable. The author is very much in tune with the concerns and sensitivities
of "the people" and offers sound theological, historical and pastoral commentary on the Eucharistic liturgy. The book can be used as the basis for seminars
or workshops for newcomers to the music group or liturgy committee.

Fr. Joseph M. Champlin
CHRIST PRESENT AND YET TO COME: The Priest and God's People at Prayer
(Maryknoll: Orbis Books, 1971) 225 pp. $2.50.

This book is invaluable for the musician serious about his or her liturgical role. We suggest it as an ideal follow-up to Fr. Dallen's *Worship in a New World.* It is serious and important reading without being "heavy." Part One deals with "The Celebrant's Attitude in a Flexible Liturgy" but is definitely worth reading by all who participate in the celebration. The second section is addressed more generally, covering parish committees and with special celebrations for penance, baptism, marriage and funerals.

Dan F. Onley
REFRESHER/WORKBOOK for the Folk Musician in Liturgy
(Cincinnati: North American Liturgy Resources, 1973) $3.95

When used in conjunction with workshop sessions, or private study of *With Lyre, Harp and a Flatpick* and other books recommended in these pages, this "Workbook" becomes a highly-useful personal reference book. Key considerations are presented in a format which encourages the reader to formulate his or her own reactions, ideas, observations, additions and suggestions — and provides space to write them down. The key points raised are those persistently encountered by the author in workshops conducted by those most active in this field. The workbook can readily serve as a framework for local educational efforts or learning sessions for other folk musicians.

Eugene S. Geissler and Kenneth W. Peters
TOGETHER AT MASS
(Notre Dame: Ave Maria Press, 1973) $2.50

Certainly an inviting and attractive book, *Together at Mass* intertwines commentary and explanation of the parts of the Mass with a series of 24 Liturgies of the Word, each of which draws attention to a particular part of the total celebration.

Fr. Lucien Deiss
THE SPIRIT AND SONG OF THE NEW LITURGY
(Cincinnati: World Library Publications, Inc., 1971) $7.95

The internationally-respected author presents a detailed study of the role of song in the Christian liturgical tradition. Recommended for those who have a foundation in both music and liturgical study.

With Lyre, Harp
and a Flatpick:
The
Folk
Musician
at
Worship

Don Schenk
THE DON SCHENK METHOD FOR GUITAR   (6 books)
— Chord Primer (Basic Chording Technique)
1. Reading Musican Notation
2. Melody in Chords
3. Music Theory
4. Fingerpicking Technique
5. Chord Manual

(Cincinnati: North American Liturgy Resources, 1972)

We recommend this particular course because we see it used and we see it
bring results. The books of the Mel Bay Method have long been the standard,
especially with teachers, but the Schenk Method turns out to be more manag-
able for the student working privately. The author is a popular and active
teacher at a large metropolitan school of music, and the texts of the books
were critically edited by guitar students. While the multitude of one-volume
how-to books available can certainly give helpful pointers, the Don Schenk
series excels in its graded approach, clearness and comprehensiveness.

Joe Wise
THE BODY AT LITURGY
(Cincinnati: North American Liturgy Resources, 1972). $4.95

Today's folk musicians are as visible and physically prominent as the celebrant.
Consequently, this book about style, presence and movement in the celebration
is of crucial concern to the musician. Joe Wise's experience as a folk musician
at worship adds to the pertinence of this general book about "bodiliness" to
musicians.

Bernard Huijbers   (Revised translation by Redmond McGoldrick SJ)
THE PERFORMING AUDIENCE: Vernacular Liturgy and
Musical Style
(Cincinnati: North American Liturgy Resources, 1972, 1974) $3.95

NEW EDITION. A limited first printing of this work was swiftly sold out in
1972. The revised translation already promises to play an important role in
guiding the development of new liturgical music in America. Of special interest to the folk musician is the author's insights into the true nature of *Volks
Musik* and his critical appraisal of the role of "formal" music in worship. He
offers a fresh perspective on what congregational singing is really all about.

Bishops' Committee on the Liturgy
MUSIC IN CATHOLIC WORSHIP
(1972: U. S. Catholic Conference, 1312 Massachusetts Ave. N.W.,
    Washington, D.C. 20005)

As we suggested in Chapter Nine, this booklet is an absolute must for us all. The booklet by itself, or in conjunction with other resources mentioned, can be the basis for very fruitful further education of the parish music group. U.S.C.C. publications are occasionally stocked by religious book dealers or religious education or liturgy offices; otherwise, request it directly.

Notes

Notes

Notes

CREDITS:

Design and Editorial Preparation: DAN ONLEY and DAVE SEREY
Cover Design: MIKE ZWERTSCHEK
Illustrations: DAVE SIMMONS
Typesetting: NATALIE WAUGH

PHOTOGRAPHS: Ed Gutfreund, Mike Zwertschek, Dan Onley, Cincinnati *Post/Times-Star* (Mimi Fuller, p. 136), Leo Santiago, Ray Schuhmann (p. 113).